MEDIEVAL LOGIC AND
METAPHYSICS

D1245420

Philosophy

Editor

PROFESSOR S. KÖRNER
jur.Dr., Ph.D., F.B.A.

Professor of Philosophy
University of Bristol and Yale University

MEDIEVAL LOGIC AND METAPHYSICS

A MODERN INTRODUCTION

D. P. Henry

Reader in Philosophy
in the University of Manchester

HUTCHINSON UNIVERSITY LIBRARY

LONDON

HUTCHINSON & CO (*Publishers*) **LTD**

3 Fitzroy Square, London W1

London Melbourne Sydney Auckland
Wellington Johannesburg Cape Town
and agencies throughout the world

First published 1972

*This book has been set in Times type, printed in Great Britain
on smooth wove paper by William Clowes & Sons Limited
London, Colchester and Beccles, and bound by
Wm. Brendon & Son Limited, Tiptree, Essex*

ISBN 0 09 110830 6 (cased)
0 09 110831 4 (paper)

NON TANTUM DEBEMUS
INHAERERE IMPROPRIETATI VERBORUM VERITATEM
TEGENTI QUANTUM
INHIARE PROPRIETATI VERITATIS
SUB
MULTIMODO GENERE LOCUTIONUM
LATENTI

*We ought not to be
held back by the way
in which the improprieties
of speech hide the truth,
but should rather aspire
to the precision of the
truth which lies hidden
under the multiplicity
of ways of talking*

(St Anselm of Canterbury,
De Casu Diaboli)

CONTENTS

PREFACE

When Columbus was arguing that it should be possible to sail west-wards in order to encounter India, he ran into the opposition of pedants who were themselves no navigators. In their comfortable studies, armed with a vested interest in the prejudices of vague and wildly approximate knowledge, they claimed to know in advance the impossibility of what long and laborious voyages later proved to be the case. It would appear that much of philosophy is still in the stage at which the anti-Columbians found themselves: there is much talk about logic, but little actual logic; there is much vague and approximate chat adorned with high-sounding terminology and perhaps a few logical-looking squiggles, yet little appreciation of what an actual deduction in a forward-looking system of philosophical logic might be like. And although this book is overtly concerned with sample soundings from only one comparatively unsurveyed ocean, the suggestions which it is intended to convey are of quite general import: patience and laborious voyages may be necessary before solid and established claims can be laid to philosophical progress.

Contentment with remaining at the stage of preliminary approximation carries with it the danger of a running-together of cases which, upon further exploration, turn out to be totally distinct. It has been suggested that the earlier cartographers of Columbus' newly-found island of Hispaniola were prone to endow it with the shape and attitude which previous and speculative charts had attributed to Zipangu (Japan). If one's exploration cannot but remain sketchy and incomplete, then this sort of hasty running-together of vaguely-resembling items is only to be expected. Consider, for instance, the vast amount of material, disparate to a quite high degree, which a present-day philosopher might be prepared to bring under a heading such as 'Identity'; cases which upon exploration turn out to have little in common save the nominal possibility of being brought under this single title are enumerated and settled together, almost all in the same breath.

What is needed now is analogous to what was needed at the time of Columbus: patient and minute surveys of the actual terrain, backed up by accurate instruments and charts. This requires time, patience, cooperation and communication. Although in its detail of a comparatively humdrum nature, with few fireworks and only an aesthetic charm residing in calm and measured rigour (as opposed to the dramatic emotional appeal of arm-chair architectonics), such exploration at least promises progress in philosophy; one minute truth is more of an acquisition than myriads of ungrounded speculations.

The indebtedness of the present work to the writings and conversation of Czeslaw Lejewski will be evident from the many references to his studies which are herein made. Part II is, in effect, an elementary digest of certain of those studies, and I have endeavoured at every point to supply information as to the nature of my sources in his works. He has helped me to purge that part of inaccuracies and inelegances; for those which subsist therein or elsewhere, I alone am responsible. Staff and students at the universities of Manchester and Pennsylvania, as well as friends at various other universities in Britain, USA and Canada, have also, by their discussions and remarks, assisted in the task of sharpening, shaping, and trimming—a process which is doubtless still incomplete.

Acknowledgements are due to the editors of *The Notre Dame Journal of Formal Logic, Franciscan Studies, Analecta Anselmiana,* and *Logique et Analyse* (cf. no. 27, Oct. 1964) for permission to exploit portions of articles of mine which have appeared in their publications. I am also indebted to F. S. Schmitt, N. Kretzmann, The Pontifical Institute of Medieval Studies (Toronto), The Franciscan Institute (St Bonaventure), and L. M. De Rijk for kindly allowing me to reproduce portions of the text of the works of St Anselm, William of Sherwood, Walter Burleigh, and Abelard which they have edited, translated, or published, and to David Mannings for permission to use his 'Hume and a Broom'. Finally, and by no means least because last-mentioned, there is my indebtedness to Stephan Körner, who as editor is responsible for the very existence of this volume. Without his kind suggestions and help it would not have been produced.

D.P.H.

Department of Philosophy,
University of Manchester

Spring 1971

REFERENCES AND ABBREVIATIONS

Cross-references to the numbered sections of the text are preceded by the number of the relevant Part (I, II, or III) when reference is being made from one Part to another; otherwise the cross-reference is internal to the Part in which it occurs. The section-number may also have annexed to it the number of one of the expressions which occurs within it, as when 'II §3.1.9' is used to refer to the expression numbered '.9' within §3.1 of Part II.

Titles of books and articles referred to are abbreviated as follows:

ACG	Aquinas, Thomas (St)	Summa contra Gentiles
AD	Abelard, Peter	Dialectica (Ed. L. M. De Rijk, 1956)
AP	Geyer, B. (Ed.)	Peter Abelard's Philosophische Schriften (*Beitrage zur Geschichte der Philosophie und Theologie des Mittelalters*, vol. XXI, 1919–1933)
APH	Aquinas, Thomas (St)	Commentary on *Peri Hermeneias* (Ed. Spiazzi, 1955)
AST	Aquinas, Thomas (St)	Summa Theologiae
B	Boethius	Opera Omnia: Tomus Posterior (Migne)
BDP	Burleigh, Walter	De Puritate Artis Logicae (Ed. P. Boehner, 1955)
BH	Bocheński, I. M.	A History of Formal Logic (Tr. I. Thomas, 1961)
BML	Boehner, P.	Medieval Logic (1952)
DLM	De Rijk, L.M.	Logica Modernorum, vol. I (1962), vol. II (1967)
GRG	Geach, P. T.	Reference and Generality (1962)
HAN	Henry, D. P.	St Anselm's Nonsense (*Mind*, Jan. 1963)

HDG	Henry, D. P.	The *De Grammatico* of St Anselm (1964)
HL	Henry, D. P.	The Logic of St Anselm (1967)
HW	Henry, D. P.	Why '*Grammaticus*'? (*Archivum Latinitatis Medii Aevi*, vol. XXVIII, fasc. 2–3)
JL	Joseph, H. W. B.	An Introduction to Logic (2nd ed. 1916)
KDL	Kneale, W. & M.	Development of Logic (1962)
LAS	Lejewski, C.	Proper Names (*Aristotelian Society*, Supplementary vol. XXI)
LCM	Lejewski, C.	Consistency of Leśniewski's Mereology (*Journal of Symbolic Logic*, vol. 34, 1969)
LE	Locke, John	Essay Concerning Human Understanding
LLE	Lejewski, C.	Logic and Existence (*British Journal for the Philosophy of Science*, 1954)
LLL	Luschei, E. C.	The Logical Systems of Leśniewski (1962)
LM	Lejewski, C.	A contribution to Leśniewski's Mereology (*Year Book of Polish Society of Arts and Sciences Abroad*, vol. 5, 1955)
LR	Lejewski, C.	On Leśniewski's Ontology (*Ratio*, vol. I, 1958)
LTD	Lejewski, C.	A re-examination of the Russellian Theory of Descriptions (*Philosophy*, vol. XXV, 1960)
MMC	Moody, E. A.	The Medieval Contribution to Logic (*Studium Generale*, vol. 19, 1966)
MOS	Matthews, G. B.	Ockham's Supposition Theory and Modern Logic (*Philosophical Review*, Jan. 1964)
OSL	Ockham, William of	Summa Logicae, Pars Prima (Ed. P. Boehner, 1951)
QDE	Quine, W. V.	Designation and Existence (*Journal of Philosophy*, vol. 36, 1939)
QF	Quine, W. V.	From a Logical Point of View (1953)
QML	Quine, W. V.	Mathematical Logic (1947)
RI	Russell, B.	Introduction to Mathematical Philosophy (1919)

S	Schmitt, F. S. (Ed.)	S. Anselmi Opera Omnia, vol. I
SA	Sobociński, B.	L'analyse de l'antinomie Russellienne par Leśniewski (*Methodos*, vols. I & II)
SM	Sobociński, B.	Studies in Leśniewski's Mereology (*Year Book of Polish Society of Arts and Sciences Abroad*, vol. 5, 1955)
TLO	Trentman, J.	Leśniewski's Ontology and some Medieval Logicians (*Notre Dame Journal of Formal Logic*, vol. X, 1969)
WSS	Sherwood, William of	Treatise on Syncategorematic Words (Tr. N. Kretzmann, 1968)
WST	Sherwood, William of	The *Syncategoremata* of William of Sherwood (Ed. J. R. O'Donnell, *Mediaeval Studies*, vol. II, 1941)

Part I

INTRODUCTION

§1 MEDIEVAL PHILOSOPHY AND MEDIEVAL LOGIC

There is a clear and salient contrast between the state of the history of medieval philosophy and that of the history of medieval logic. The first is an already-venerable discipline, and has customarily been the province of thinkers who themselves are part of the post-medieval phase of philosophising, literary in mode, and remote in style and content from the logically-structured and economically-expressed output of the medievals. The second, the history of medieval logic, is a comparatively new study, which according to the avowals of its own practitioners is still in an elementary and primitive state. There are, however, at least a couple of reasons why the further development of the history of medieval logic would appear to be of the very highest interest. In the first place, there is no doubt that the concerns of medieval logicians and philosophers were often closer to those of contemporary philosophers than to those of philosophers who lived in the intervening centuries, given the current concern with problems of language and meaning. It is already clear that an intelligible conversation between medieval logicians and modern philosophers could be quite profitable. In the second place, given the already-mentioned logical complexion of medieval philosophising in general, a result of such a conversation could be a fuller understanding of that philosophising, particularly in its more metaphysical stretches. Such a result would scarcely be surprising in view of the literary and non-logical cast of mind of most of those who have hitherto taken upon themselves the study of the history of medieval thought. Another concomitant result would be a more unified perspective of medieval thought as a whole, carrying with it the possibility of settled and conclusive verdicts on the nature and content of that thought in some of its aspects.

1

§2   MEDIEVAL LOGIC AND MODERN LOGIC

At this point the question may well be raised as to the extent to which
contemporary studies of medieval logic are capable of fulfilling the
sort of promise outlined above. Medieval logic was a philosophical
logic, closely geared to philosophical themes. What then could a
purely formalist logic, interested purely in combinations of uninterpreted notation, have in common with medieval logic? Again, assuming that this first difficulty may be obviated by the use of a non-
formalist type of modern logic, the fact still remains that both in logic
and metaphysics the medievals used a highly systematised Latin,
extremely rich and daring in its proliferation of forms of speech
belonging to recondite semantical categories. How then is it possible
for a philosophical formal logic of the current sort in this respect to
rival and exceed (as it must) the medieval artificialised language?
Finally, the medievals were blithely uninhibited by any of the dark
and knotty controversies which have arisen as a result of our contemporary entanglement of the notion of existence with the device
central to modern formal logic, namely the device of quantification
(cf. II §2). How then can modern logic, caught as it is in this entangle-
ment, recapture the untrammelled approach to existence enjoyed by
its medieval predecessors?

So far, only questions of broad principle have been raised, but it
is not difficult to raise doubts at the level of the details of down-to-
earth analysis of medieval theories. Already in *BML* a certain uneasiness had been voiced (*BML* 28–31, *BML* 44; cf. III §3). These
doubts were made more explicit in *MMC*, and one way of spelling
out the nature of one of them arises from the different ways in which
a propositional form of the type in which the medievals were interested
can be analysed. Let it be premised that a *name* and a *predicate*
or *verb*, i.e. a form which when completed by a (proper) name constitutes a proposition (assertive sentence), are diverse parts of speech.
Now as is made clear in *RI* 162, for instance, it is considered by some
modern logicians that the correct analysis of a sentence such as 'All
men are mortal' would run 'For no matter what *x*, if *x* is a man,
then *x* is mortal', wherein '*x*' is a variable for proper names. But now
it is evident that the 'men' and 'mortal' parts of the original sentence,
parts which would be considered as names (taking 'name' to comprise
adjectives as well as common and proper nouns), have the predicates
'... is a man' and '... is mortal' as their counterparts in the modern
analysis.

However, the medievals, although aware of this possibility of the
'predicatisation' of names (*BML* 28, 30), would still wish to view 'man'

and 'mortal' as names and not predicates, or at any rate would not 'construe both terms of a general categorical proposition as predicate terms' (*MMC* 448). Now in some other segments of the more familiar modern logic it is still possible to take 'man' and 'mortal' to be names, but they then turn out to be the proper names of entities called 'classes', i.e. 'All men are mortal' is construed as 'The whole of the class of men is included in the class of mortal beings'; this is plainly alien to the point of the original assertion, which many of the medievals would take to be about men and mortal beings, and not about the inter-relationships of two further class-entities. In Moody's terms, 'the medieval logician did not construe the terms of such propositions as singular names of classes, but as general names of individuals' (*MMC* 449).

At the present juncture, therefore, in the light of these remarks and others which will be cited in III §1, it would appear that explanations in ordinary language, with only rare and occasional help from the language of formal logic in comparatively uninteresting contexts, is the most that can be expected of the history of medieval logic. Under these circumstances the promise of the sort of definitive conclusions which formal logical analysis would provide concerning the sense and validity of medieval logical and philosophical theses seems to be impossible of fulfilment.

Fortunately it happens that there exists a system of modern formal logic, unfamiliar to many logicians and philosophers, and sometimes misunderstood by others, which allows the investigator to overcome all of the difficulties stated above, and from the standpoint of which many of the further difficulties which may still be raised can be satisfactorily resolved. This logic is that of the Polish logician S. Leśniewski (1886–1939), a partial account of which may be found in Part II below. This logic is anti-formalist, in that its theorems are interpreted truths, and not mere syntactically-permissible combinations of uninterpreted marks (cf. II §0.00). It has the capacity for the introduction of indefinitely many new parts of speech (semantical categories) and hence can adapt itself to the required degree of exactitude for the purpose of analysing medieval logic, as Part III will demonstrate. It employs an interpretation of the quantifiers which allows dissociation of the latter from its usually necessary entangle-ment with the notion of existence (II §2.23, II §2.25), and so is in a position to come to more exact terms with medieval discourse on this topic.

It follows that the purpose of the present work is three-fold. After the preliminary consideration of the field which is contained in this introduction, a practical account of one of the central theories of Leśniewski, namely his *Ontology*, will be presented in Part II. Thus

2

armed, we will be in a position to expose in detail in Part III some examples of the way in which Ontology may be used in the analysis of medieval themes.

Now this may all sound to be a formidable undertaking for those readers who are no logicians, and they may feel tempted to remain at the level of analyses and explanations conducted in everyday language, with perhaps a few elementary terms or scraps of notation from current logic or linguistics thrown in. Indeed, there may be some who in spite of their own logical competence are as yet unconvinced of the value of making a text intelligible in the light of a fully systematised language, and who would protest that if intelligibility cannot be offered by explanation in terms of comparatively ordinary language, then so much the worse for the medievals who insist on being unintelligible in this way. To such objection three types of reply are possible. First, efforts have been made in Part II to give an explanation of Leśniewski's Ontology, with which we are to be mainly concerned, of so elementary a nature as to be easily grasped by all who have only the slightest acquaintance with the logic of propositions and the notion of quantification. Secondly, as has already been contended above, the highly systematised technical logical Latin of the medievals involved the introduction of new parts of speech which stand outside the elucidatory capacities of ordinary language. Thirdly, even if ordinary language is itself artificialised somewhat in the medieval sort of style, there are limits to its intelligibility unless the analysis is carried forward into a fully systematic language such as that of Ontology. Partly in support of this contention an effort will now be made to give a preliminary appreciation and survey of the nature of themes which are to be touched upon in Part III. In the course of this effort ordinary language will be strained to the uttermost in order to come to terms with the way in which the scholastics modified such language for technical purposes. Even this straining will, in the end, be found wanting; this will convey concretely the necessity of going yet further, to the fully artificial language outlined in Part II.

§3   PRELIMINARY SURVEY

It is to the ill-fated Boethius, who died by the order of a barbarian emperor in the year A.D. 524, that our segment of the history of logic chiefly owes its origin. His grandiose plan had been to translate into Latin and elucidate the works of the ancient Greek philosophers. In point of fact he accomplished only the translation of Aristotle's logical works, along with commentaries on some of them, as well as some monographs based on Aristotelian and Stoic sources. Only some of these were available to early medieval logicians, such as St Anselm (1033–1109), the 'father of Scholasticism'; thus he would know Boethius' version of Aristotle's *Categoriae* and *De Interpretatione*, along with Boethian commentaries on these and on the *Isagoge* of the neo-Platonist Porphyry; Boethius' own works on the categorical and hypothetical syllogism were also known at this time. Only later, however, did Aristotle's *Analytica* (prior and posterior), *Topica*, and *De Sophisticis Elenchis* afford meat for the busy minds of medieval logicians (cf. *DLM, KDL, BH*).

Nevertheless, the judgement of the seventeenth-century English philosopher John Locke could already have St Anselm as one of its targets. For when Locke accuses the schoolmen of having 'covered their ignorance with a curious and inexplicable web of perplexed words', he touches upon one of the essential and generally-admitted characteristics of much medieval philosophy and logic of which Anselm was already acutely conscious, namely its progressive systematisation of the Latin in which it is written. At times this systematisation goes over the boundaries of sense into what is, from the point of view of ordinary, pre-technical discourse, nonsense (cf. III §2).

In order to achieve a concrete appreciation of what is involved here, as well as a preview of some of the problems to be investigated in Part III, consider a systematisation of ordinary English (call it 'S-English', 'system-English') which incorporates functors (i.e. incomplete expressions which when completed by one or more expressions of appropriate semantical category constitute an expression belonging to a definite semantical category) whereby a *name* may be formed from any *verb*, thus:

.1   {   }er   (cf. II §5.15)

and a verb from any name, thus:

.2   (   )ise   (cf. II §5.16, .17, .18)

By filling the gap in .1 with a verb one forms a name, as when from 'think' one has '{think}er'. By filling the gap in .2 with a name one forms a verb, as when from 'deputy' one has '(deputy)ise' (in ordinary English 'deputise'). The brackets enclosing the gaps show by their shape to which semantical category (e.g. verb, name) the completing expression should belong. Such completing expressions are termed the 'arguments' of the functor which they complete. Note that the term 'name' as herein used covers the grammarian's proper names, common nouns, adjectives and other name-like expressions (cf. II §1).

In a similar vein one can have a functor incorporating the verb 'is' which, when completed by two names, forms a sentence, thus:

.3   (   ) is (   )   (cf. II §2.211)

As in .2 the brackets here indicate nominal arguments as appropriate, so that '(Socrates) is (king)' shows appropriate arguments for the completion of .3. Again, one can have a functor likewise incorporating the verb 'is', but which takes as completing arguments two *verbs*, as opposed to the names appropriate in .3, i.e.

.4   {   } is {   }   (cf. II §5.19)

As in .1, the curly brackets here indicate verb-completion, so that appropriate arguments are displayed in sentences such as '{Think} is {cogitate}' and '{Idealise} is {generalise}' (in ordinary English 'To think is to cogitate', 'To idealise is to generalise', or 'Thinking is cogitating', 'Idealising is generalising').

We now have the elements of a systematic language incorporating a universal noun–verb correlation, two senses of 'is', and which can be used as a rough model against which to measure the medieval systematisations. This model is in its turn a crude version of some of the functors which occur in the fully artificial language—the Ontology of Leśniewski—which will be described in Part II and exploited in Part III.

For present purposes I postulate (following C. Lejewski) that abstract nouns are in fact more verb-like than name-like (cf. III, §5.11, .12, §6.18). Some of the medievals implicitly or overtly recognised this kinship, e.g. Anselm of Canterbury and Thomas Aquinas (*c.* 1224–74) (cf. III §2, §6). Now if we have a Latin language in which every name (including the grammarian's adjective) has its abstract correlate (as 'white' has 'whiteness', and 'man' 'humanity') then given the postulate mentioned, that language (call it 'S-Latin') will have reproduced something like the verb–name correlation available in S-English. Neither Boethius nor Anselm of Canterbury appear to have assumed such a complete correlation; the later medievals, as Locke reminds us, were quick to remedy this incompleteness (*LE* III 8 §2, *HL* §3.131).

Several further types of systematic uniformity are now possible in S-Latin. Thus, consider the sentences *Socrates currit* 'Socrates runs' and *Socrates est albus* 'Socrates is white'. In the first case the verb or predicate *currit* 'runs' is simple, and in the second complex (*est albus* 'is white'). Boethius, following Aristotle, recognised that the first could be made to have the same structure as the second by being restated as *Socrates est currens* 'Socrates is (a) runner' (*B* 348D). But now, switching for a moment to the S-English versions of these sentences, it is plain that in 'runner' we have a name formed from

a verb. Is there any way of getting a similar effect in both the Latin
and English versions of the second sentence (*Socrates est albus*
'Socrates is white')? Let us consider the S-English case first. We can
easily, by .2, form the verb '(white)ise' from 'white', and then by .1
nominalise the result, obtaining '{(white)ise}er'. Under these circumstances both 'Socrates is a runner' and 'Socrates is white' can be
reduced to structural uniformity, since when the second becomes
'Socrates is a {(white)ise}er', both can be seen to be instances of the
S-English functor:

.5   (   ) is ({   }er)   (cf. .3, .1 and II §5.15)

If we concentrate on the second argument of the 'is' of .5 a partly
similar process can also be imagined in respect of S-Latin, thanks
to the universal correlation between names and abstract nouns mentioned above. To make it work here we must combine the abstract
noun with the verb *habere* 'to have', as in *albedinem habens* 'whiteness-
haver', *humanitatem habens* 'humanity-haver', and so on, in which
we obtain, for instance, the nominal form {*albedinem-hab*}*ens* '{white-
ness-hav}er' from the 'verb' *albedinem-hab* 'whiteness-hav'. From all
this it in turn emerges, given the full availability of abstract nouns,
that the transformation just described incorporates a fashion in which
all names can be seen as having a uniform structure, thus:

(a)	(b)	(c)
white	whiteness-hav-er	{(white)ise}er
albus	*albedinem-hab-ens*	
man	humanity-hav-er	{(man)ise}er
homo	*humanitatem-hab-ens*	
gold	goldness-hav-er	{(gold)ise}er
aurum	*aureitatem-hab-ens*	

Column (a) shows the name, (b) the exploitation of the now universally
available abstract nouns to produce a uniformly-structured S-Latin
correlate (with English translation) of the S-English forms of (c). This
generality could be elaborated still further in a way indicated by
Aquinas: the *-hab-ens* '-hav-er' of column (b) can be varied to give
analogous senses of the names, as when 'healthy' could be constructed
not merely as 'health-hav-er' but also as 'health-caus-er' (e.g. when
used of medicine) or as 'health-signifi-er' (e.g. when used of a good
complexion) *AST* I, q. 13, art. 5. This elaboration need not, however,
be pursued here.

   And now, using functors .1 and .2 as a means of recognising noun-
fillable verb-forms and verb-fillable noun-forms one might rise above
the endless list of S-English concrete cases available (concerning gold,

men, whites, and so on), and make a generalisation relying on columns
(a) and (c) above, and having the following form:

.6   Every (   ) is a {(   )ise}er   (cf. III §6.20)

It is understood that for .6 to become a truth it must be preceded
by a phrase such as 'For all appropriate arguments', and taken to
imply a uniform filling in of the two '( )' gaps. Now in view of the
use of 'essence' as a quasi-name for such 'things' as humanity, i.e.
(man)ise, whiteness i.e. (white)ise, and so on, column (b) above
suggests that a near approach to .6 in Latin and English would be
Omne ens est essentiam habens 'Every be-er is an essence-hav-er' (cf.
III §6.16). Further, one may note that the *-ens* of the first of these
two sentences corresponds to the '-er' in the English version in a quite
remarkable way; after all, *ens* is not only the Latin for 'be-er' (or
'being' as a name), but is also the termination common to the *hab-ens*
parts of the S-Latin noun-structures listed under (b) above. It might
hence not be too fanciful to conjecture that some of the medievals,
Aquinas particularly, saw *ens* 'being' as an '{ } *ens*' corresponding
to the '{ }er' of .6 above. Should this be so, it is already clear that
ordinary-language elucidations of medieval theses on 'being', elucidations relying on our disorganised intuitions as to how the word
functions in non-technical language, will incur the danger of running
pretty wide of the mark. A first attempt to bring such material under
systematic control is presented at III §6.

Starting from foundations such as those described, the S-Latin of
the medievals becomes stretched to the limits of sense, and at times
passes over into controlled nonsense for the expression of theses which
require abnormal combinations of semantical categories, or the invention of categories quite foreign to non-technical usage. For
example, to anticipate III §6 further, we may note that Aquinas
intends to convey by his use of *esse* 'to be' the 'indivision' (i.e. the
being-exactly-one) of a thing. Now '. . . is-exactly-one' is a complex
verb, so that when we encounter the Aquinate thesis *Omne ens est
esse habens* 'Every being is an *esse*-haver' (III §6.17) we can construe
it after the pattern of the essence-sentence .6 above, but with the blank
in '{( )ise}er' now filled by the argument 'exactly-one', i.e. it becomes:

.7   Every (   ) is an {(exactly-one)ise}er   (cf. III §6.24)

Although .7 is scarcely expressible in English without nonsense, the
corresponding Latin which was quoted, although barbarous, is still
not nonsense. We do encounter nonsense, however, when it is stated
that *entia per participationem* 'beings by participation', i.e. beings
characterisable by '{( )ise}er' (in S-Latin *habens* . . . with the gap
fillable by an abstract noun or *esse*), are not their *esse*, and some of

them are not their essences; thus a man is not his essence (humanity), neither is he his *esse* (*homo nec est humanitas nec est esse suum*). One part of this denial is such that the sorts of noun exemplified by 'man' and 'humanity' just will not mix around the same 'is' (or 'is not'); we hence have a piece of what is, from the point of view of non-technical English (and correspondingly, non-technical Latin) arrant nonsense. Yet such an assertion is acceptable in S-Latin, and inferences possible therefrom. However, the other part of the denial quoted, namely that which asserts that a man's nature (humanity) is distinct from his *esse*, serves to bring out its point. For if the suggestions made above are adopted, i.e. if 'humanity' is construed as the verb '(man)ise' and *esse* as the verb '(exactly-one)ise', then it follows that this last-mentioned distinction involves the verb-completed 'is' of .4, i.e. the distinction has the form:

.8   It is not the case that: {(man)ise} is {(exactly-one)ise}

Whence we may gather that the nonsensical denials mentioned, belonging as they do to the same family, must likewise be analysed at the level of the 'is' of .4 as opposed to the 'is' of .3. 'This man is distinct from his nature (humanity)' becomes:

.9   It is not the case that: {(this-man)ise} is {(man)ise}

and 'This man is distinct from his *esse*' becomes:

.10   It is not the case that: {(this-man)ise} is {(exactly-one)ise}

Although we have now reached a point at which S-English could, on one interpretation of the '-ise' termination, be positively misleading, it is at least evident that one service which the barbarisms and nonsense under discussion render is to call attention to the fact that the semantical categories involved are unusual, in the sense that they are not, for example, the ones which a *prima facie* reading in terms of the 'is' of .3 might lead one to believe they are. Devices like nonsense, therefore, coupled with the characteristic terminations of abstract nouns and the use of the infinitive *esse* 'to be', as well as other features peculiar to the patterns of discourse here in question, perform a role rather similar to that of the '{' and '}' of '{   } is {   }'; cumulatively they signal a warning of the abnormal features of such discourse. The semi-artificial language which ensues is clumsy. That precise definitional and systematic control which goes with a totally artificial language of the sort described in Part II is lacking. Even when this lack has been partially remedied by extraordinary intuitive powers, history shows that there is no guarantee that communication will be maintained, as III §5 demonstrates when a more exact treatment of this sort of thing is provided. Such, nevertheless, is the point of the 'web of perplexed words' of which Locke speaks. In Anselm of Canterbury it is but a particular facet of his immensely pervasive realisation that the overt, apparent, or grammatical form of an utterance need not show forth its implicit, true, or logical form—a realisation re-initiated in our own age by Russell (cf. III §2, *HL* §4.012, *HAN*). Anselm frequently contrasts the forms of speech allowed by the loose texture of ordinary language (*usus loquendi*) with the forms to which a strict attention to the exact sense (*significatio per se*) commits one. The breaks with usage demanded by systematic truth-statement are displayed in sentences such as 'Literate is literacy' which in its Latin version (*Grammaticus est grammatica*) is grammatically scandalous, and there would seem to be little hope of ever making it intelligible in 'ordinary language' (cf. III §2, *HL* §3.2, and *HAN*).

Naturally the early medieval classicists, like their fellows of the sixteenth-century Renaissance, reacted against these deformations of language. Thus the *Metalogicon* of John of Salisbury (*c.* 1115–1180) explicitly argues against mixtures of abstract and concrete in the style we have been considering (cf. *HL* §2.21). But such protests failed to retard this characteristic development of medieval philosophy, and Aquinas' well-known distinction between essence and *esse*, some opening moves of which have been roughly sketched above, involves a worth-while exploitation of novel semantical categories, as III §6 attempts to show.

The breakdown in communication hinted at above is exemplified when William of Ockham (*c.* 1285–1349) criticises the *distinctio formalis a parte rei* 'thing-centred formal distinction' propounded by Duns Scotus (*c.* 1266–1308) (cf. III §5). According to Ockham the Scotists hold that in respect of an individual thing, such a distinction obtains between the 'universal' nature in question (e.g. humanity in the case of a man) and the ultimate individuating property or 'individual difference' (e.g. *Socrateitas* 'Socraticity' in the case of Socrates) which make the individual into *this* individual. Note how the correlation between common nouns and corresponding abstract nouns which was observed above as a symptom of the artificialisation of philosophical discourse has now been extended to the area of proper names also—an extension suggested centuries before by Boethius, but only finally exploited by Scotus to the extreme extent of correlating 'this' with 'thisness' (*haecceitas*) to accommodate the cases of objects which, unlike most human beings, have no proper name other than the ambiguous 'this'. Ockham cannot reconcile the fact that the distinction purports to be *a parte rei* 'thing-centred' with the Scotist claim that it does not commit its proponents to the existence of abstract entities (e.g. the 'universal' *humanity* and the 'individual difference' *Socraticity*) over and above, and distinct from, the individual objects which are presented to us by the senses. Such a commitment would be denied by the Scotists. (We are here faced with an aspect of the problem of the status of 'universals', of which more later.) In terms of S-English, however, the statement that the Socraticity of Socrates is distinct from his humanity may be pitched at the level of the verb-completed 'is' (.4 above) and analysed as:

.11   It is not the case that: {(Socrates)ise} is {(man)ise}
(cf. III §5.16)

This analysis yields a thing-centred distinction which is true (given the detailed correlate of '-ise' here appropriate) and which yet does not send one on a vain search for some extra entities to which reference is being made, as could be the case if the arguments of the 'is' were nominal; in other words, the thing-centricity of this distinction does not commit one to that Platonic realism in the matter of 'universals', of which more will be said below. But Ockham assumes and states that any distinction which holds in respect of things (called by him a 'real' distinction) can only be constituted by the negation of a sentence such as one constructed from the 'is' of .3, flanked by proper nouns. Hence when he encounters the further Scotist thesis that, although a thing-centred formal distinction holds between Socraticity and humanity (for example), it is not the case that a *real* distinction holds between the two, he assumes that 'Socraticity' and 'humanity' can be treated as a couple of names which name the same object, rather in the way that 'Tully' and 'Cicero' name the same object. The negation of a real distinction between Tully and Cicero does indeed amount to the assertion of their real identity as the same individual object; on Ockham's interpretation, therefore, the denial of a real distinction between Socraticity and humanity (cf. .11) likewise amounts to a statement of a real identity. The object of the Scotist denial, however, is surely the *nature* of the distinction: its point is to state that that distinction is not pitched at the level of names (as .11 makes clear). In other words, it would be nonsense to take .11 as being of the form:

.12   It is not the case that: ((Socrates)ise) is (man)ise
(cf. III §5.17)

From the point of view of S-English, as the brackets indicate, .12 is nonsense, since the gap-filling has here been mistakenly and inappropriately performed by verbs. Unfortunately the details of Ockham's attack are aimed at exactly this sort of non-Scotist nonsense, and wrongly assume that a real identity (i.e. one framed at the level of .3) holds between arguments of the sort shown in .11 and .12. Detailed enlargements of these points are provided in III §5.

An exactly parallel sort of mistake would arise were the assumption to be made that .8 above involves an 'is' like that of .3, whose flanking gaps take names as arguments. This is the mistake in fact made by the Ockhamist criticism of the distinction between essence and existence, of which distinction .8 is an exemplification. The criticism asserts that a distinction such as .8, implicitly and absurdly assumed by the critic to be at the level shown in .3, and hence to be a real distinction between two objects, leaves open the possibility of an omnipotent God's production of something's existence without its essence (or *vice versa*). This possibility being plainly absurd, it is concluded that the distinction which gives rise to it is likewise absurd and to be rejected.

The linguistic systematisation described above was in its turn part of an effort to resolve conceptual puzzles by reference to a satisfactory theory as to how things are and why they are as they are. This theory was basically Aristotelian, and hence involved an empiricist refusal (in the full sense of the word 'empiricist') to allow the abrogation of the pre-theoretical general picture of how things are by any theory, philosophical or otherwise. This involved the reminder that human beings as such inevitably find themselves confronted with a world populated by a multiplicity of diverse sorts and kinds of objects which are generated, develop, and perish. These objects are understood (in the sense that 'Why?' questions about them or their kinds can be answered) and are the objects of evaluation (i.e. they or their quantities, qualities, states, or relations, for example, are said to be good, bad, beautiful, ugly, and so on). The non-abrogatory policy mentioned demanded a technical vocabulary such that this pre-theoretical picture does not forfeit its basic sense by relativisation to a supposedly more fundamental picture. Thus, for example, place must always be left for the attribution of a literal (and not merely metaphorical) sense to questions as to the makings of observed objects or processes. The notion of 'matter' represents an attempt to guarantee such a sense —it was for the Aristotelian the general reply to the always sensibly-askable question (in the context mentioned) 'What is it *made out of* ?' The detailed replies to such a question, replies such as 'Wood', 'Stone', 'Bones and flesh', 'People', 'Clay', 'Cloth', and so forth, all mention makings, materials, stuff, *out of which* something is made.

Contrasted with *matter* in this sense is the notion of *form*. The latter underpins the fact that explanations as to why things are as they are can to some extent be given by reference to the kinds or sorts to which those things belong, e.g. 'Horses are self-moving because they are animals, and all animals are self-moving'. Here a feature of a particular sort of being (horse) is explained by reference to its general kind (animal). It is the notion of *form* which, along with its alternative medieval vocabulary ('nature', 'essence', 'quiddity'), represents a reminder of the fact that things fall into distinguishable sorts (*species*) which can in turn be subsumed under broader kinds (*genera*). Since truistic explanations can be given in terms of sorts or kinds, the form or essence is said to be the principle of the intelligibility or 'explanation-worthiness' of things. General definitions such as '*Man* is a *rational animal*' stand at the basis of such explanations, and are said to hold true in respect of the *formal* (as opposed to the material) aspect of things. Roughly speaking, this formal aspect, in respect of most medieval philosophers, can be interpreted as corresponding to that level of discourse which centres round the verb-flanked 'is' of .4 above (cf. II §5.19). Thus one might say that a horse is an *equinising* or {(horse)ise}ing of its matter, a stone is a petrifying or {(stone)ise}ing of its matter, and so on.

Whether or not the definitions mentioned above are true of things in a scientific sense is of little import to the point of the notion of *form*; its point is to ensure a philosophical reflection of the many-sortedness and potential intelligibility of things; this explains why Aquinas feels himself able to state his agnosticism as to the scientific value of such definitions. Further, it is plain that in such definitional contexts the '*man*' of the technical sentence '*Man* is a species' (for example) is not of the same part of speech as the name 'man' in 'Socrates is a man'; if it were, then, as Boethius had observed, one should be able to use the two sentences mentioned as premisses whence 'Socrates is a species' could be inferred, and this would be an undesirable conclusion. How, then, are such terms as 'man', 'animal', 'genus' and 'species' as they occur in sentences like '*Man* is a species', '*Animal* is a genus' and '*Man* is *animal*' to be understood? These are sentences of a sort which must occur in the discussion of the principles of those definitions which have been described above as efforts to do justice to the *formal* aspect of things, and should accordingly be parsed in terms of completions of the verb-flanked 'is' of .4 above (cf. *LAS* 248–9 and III §6 below). If, on the contrary, such sentences are taken to consist of two *names* joined by 'is' in the style of .3, then naturally one is landed with the question, transmitted by Boethius when commenting on Porphyry, as to what the things are which these names name; for instance, are the things named by such specific or generic names abstract extra-mental entities or 'natures' such as 'animality' or 'humanity' over and above, additional to, the individual human beings and animals? An affirmative answer to this question represents one medieval form of the option for a Platonic 'realist' position in the problem of universals (cf. *LAS* 236), and throughout the period thinkers were divided on this topic.

Certain early medieval anti-realists, such as Roscelin and Garland the Computist, developed a solution which had been suggested by

Boethius; words like 'species' and 'genus', said the latter, may be interpreted as *nominum nomina* 'names of names', so that '*Man* is a species' should be analysed as '"*Man*" is a species', with 'species' here naming the word 'man', and indicating that it is predicable specifically of many individuals (*B* 176D); herein lies one of the roots of the logical doctrine developed during the thirteenth and fourteenth centuries, namely the doctrine of *suppositio* (cf. III §1). The anti-realists mentioned went further than Boethius, and regarded 'man' in '*Man* is a species' not as a mentioned name (i.e. a mentioned *significant* utterance) but as a *mere* utterance (*vox*) undergoing mention, so that we find St Anselm accusing Roscelin of having reduced universals to the 'breath of an utterance' (*flatus vocis*); cf. *HL* §3.32. On the other hand, elucidation of the meaning of specific or generic names in terms of entities in the mind ('intentions', 'concepts', and so forth) leads to the position according to which the universal is a natural (as opposed to a merely conventional) mental sign. (cf. Ockham's interpretation of simple *suppositio* mentioned in III §1 below.)

It may also be noted that matter was said by some to be the *principle of individuation* whereby form, the principle of intelligibility and (in view of its usual association with shared names) of generality, is contracted and made concrete in the particularity of the various individual 'thisnesses' which belong to a given sort. However, as Scotus recognised, the attribution of this function to matter leaves the individual as such lacking in total intelligibility, and even makes problematical the possibility of an omniscient being's (i.e. God's) radical understanding of the individual object. It was in order to overcome this difficulty that (as already noted) he formed abstract nouns from unshared names as well as from shared names, thereby allowing the supposition that individuation is performed not by a material, but by a formal principle, e.g. Socraticity, thisness, and so forth, which are of the '(   )ise' form proposed above. Again, rejection of the ways of talking appropriate to material beings and the adoption of types of discourse operating at a purely formal level, as in .8, .9, .10 above, endowed philosopher-theologians with ways of speaking about beings which are 'pure forms', as in Aquinate angelology, or about God. For example, replacement of 'man' by 'god' in .9 and .10, and the removal of the negation 'it is false that' in each case turns those assertions into truths of God-lore.

Such then is the general nature of the field which is to be investigated in detail at some sample points in Part III of the present work. In the course of this survey it has become evident that even the fairly extreme modification of the natural languages involved has failed to make explicit the finer points of sense needed for the detailed expression and control of the truths with which the medievals were concerned. The very history of their disputes confirms this suspicion. In order, therefore, to survey this field with an accuracy unavailable in modified natural language, medieval or modern, finer tools are necessary. It is to the preparation of these that Part II will be devoted.

Plainly, the use of such finer tools need not be confined to the merely historical analyses exemplified in Part III. These in fact constitute an exhibition of a way in which logic can contribute to the discussion of perennial metaphysical problems. It so happens that the medievals present us with comparatively lapidary statements of such problems, and therefore afford a peculiarly valuable starting point for their study in this new way. It is in this fashion that the scope of the present work may be seen as extending outwards, beyond the historical limits which its main subject-matter might appear to entail.

Part II

ONTOLOGY

§0.00 In accordance with the policy outlined in I §2, the logical systems of Leśniewski, including his Ontology, are to be taken as consisting of an interpreted language. Hence theses occurring in the deductive theory of Ontology are true propositions, and this not in some special or peculiar sense of 'true' appropriate only to logic, but in the same sense as that in which empirical propositions of the sciences are true. Ontology presupposes propositional calculus (called by Leśniewski 'Prototetic'). In Prototetic expressions associated with the semantical category of propositions are the central concern, whereas names, or name-like expressions inspire the inner structure of the truths of Ontology. The latter, from the point of view of its subject-matter, is a general theory of what there is, or of things in general, or even, if the antique expression is preferred, of *being as such*. The vocabulary for the expression of theses belonging to this theory must first be learned, so that truths of which we are already aware may be formulated. Such truths may then be embodied in the axiomatised system of Ontology which is to be described below.

§0.01 It follows that we must begin with a consideration of what is to count as a name. The specifications suggested below are tentative, and ultimately demand enlargement. However, the general intention will, it is hoped, be clear. Names, as hereunder described, are taken in a sense wider than that which is customary in current logic. This sense is probably closer to the usual pre-logical conception; its breadth is such that one can, when required, conveniently define in terms of it the narrower conceptions which are to be found in other logics.

§ 1   NAMES (cf. LTD 17)

§1.1 The notions of *functor* and *argument* have already been introduced in I §3. Given that a functor is an incomplete expression

16

which when completed by an expression of appropriate semantical category, constitutes an expression of a definite semantical category, then one might, following Kotarbiński, suggest the following definition: a name (or noun-expression) is an expression suitable to occur as the argument of one or other or both of the following proposition-forming functors:

.1   There exists exactly one object which is (a, an) . . .
.2   There exist at least two objects each of which is (a, an) . . .

(Note that the specification mentions only 'suitability'; the arguments need not make the functors into true propositions. Further, the word 'object' is ambiguous; as, however, the means for bringing that ambiguity under systematic control will later be available, this presents no insuperable difficulty.) The following are examples of names (or noun-expressions) which fulfil the specification given:

> Plato
> Pegasus
> unicorn
> the unicorn in the London Zoo
> midwife
> the philosopher who wrote the *Republic*
> author of *Waverley*
> the author of *Waverley*
> present king of France
> the present king of France
> the inhabitant of London who owns Buckingham Palace
> Scotch
> bald
> wise
> black

§1.2   From the above it is evident that noun-expressions can be divided into at least two sorts: those which are *simple* and those which are *compound*. The former consist of one word (a name) only, and have no parts which are either names or expressions of some other semantical category; the latter consist of more than one word, their parts being either names or expressions of some non-nominal semantical category.

§1.3   It further follows that noun-expressions may (i) designate one object only (e.g. 'Socrates'), (ii) designate more than one object (e.g. 'man'), or (iii) designate no objects (e.g. 'square circle',

'Pegasus'). One may accordingly schematise the sorts of names as follows:

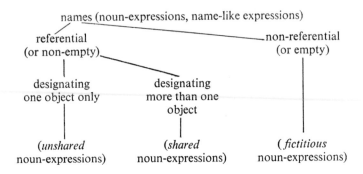

§2 FUNCTORS AND QUANTIFICATION:
INFORMAL EXPOSITION (cf. LR 54–9)

§2.1   The present remarks, intended as *ad hoc* aids in learning the vocabulary of Ontology, stand quite outside Ontology itself. At this point *any* means is good which serves its purpose. Hence any theoretical objections to those means, objections based on considerations deriving from what can sensibly be said about names and their referents, would be totally beside the point, as far as Ontology is concerned. If anyone does not understand the gist of what now follows, then the present method of introduction has failed to have an impact as far as they are concerned. If, however, understanding is provided, but exception is taken to some of the features of the aids used, this is no matter. Like Wittgenstein's ladder, the present means can be cast on one side, once they have served their purpose (cf. III §1).

§2.11   One informal and pre-systematic way of introducing the reader to the sense of certain constant terms which occur in Ontology is by means of an extension of the familiar diagrams of Euler into an *Ontological Table* (or *Table of Extension*). Thus, given the division of names into unshared, shared, and fictitious (cf. §1.3), a small shaded circle will be used to represent the only object named by an unshared name, a larger unshaded circle to represent the many objects each of which is named by a shared name, and no circle at all will correspond to a fictitious name. Diagrams I.1, I.2, and I.3 below illustrate the semantical possibilities of a single name or name-like expression, whereas diagrams II.1 to II.16 illustrate the possibilities of a pair of such expressions.

§2.12 Ontological Table

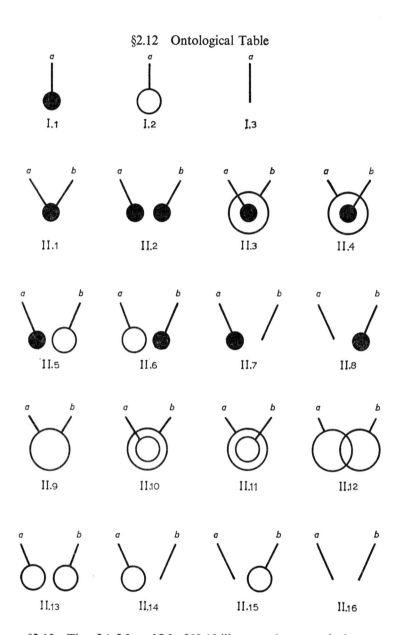

§2.13 Thus I.1, I.2, and I.3 of §2.12 illustrate the semantical status of names which are unshared, shared, and fictitious respectively. Cases II.1 and II.2 are those in which two unshared noun-expressions are

3

considered; in the first case both designate the same object, in the second each designates a different object. II.3 covers the case of such pairs as the one consisting of 'the Moon' and 'heavenly body'. The shaded circle in II.3 is then inside the unshaded one to remind us that the only object named by the name 'the Moon' happens to be one of the many objects each of which is named by the name 'heavenly body'. II.4 illustrates the converse of II.3. Examples of the remaining cases may be briefly outlined as follows (in each case the first noun-expression given in the example is taken to correspond to the '*a*' of the diagram, and the second to the '*b*'):

II.5	'Socrates'	'bird'
II.6	Converse of II.5	
II.7	'Socrates'	'square circle'
II.8	Converse of II.7	
II.9	'man'	'rational animal'
II.10	'philosopher'	'man'
II.11	Converse of II.10	
II.12	'coin'	'that which is made of gold'
II.13	'man'	'bird'
II.14	'man'	'centaur'
II.15	Converse of II.14	
II.16	'mermaid'	'centaur'

§2.14   The diagrams given above may now be used to determine the meaning of certain functors which form propositions from one or from two nominal arguments. This determination, informal and preliminary though it be, is nevertheless a step from the variety of sense possible in pre-theoretical usage to a fixed and technical sense appropriate to Ontology. In the same way as physicists, lawyers, engineers, and stockbrokers (for instance) make new and exact uses of old terms drawn from non-technical language, so also here precision and technical sense is suggested for already familiar words. Hence there is no claim here that the senses suggested exhaust or uniquely analyse corresponding expressions of ordinary talk. On the contrary, *some* senses of the latter may be as it were measured in terms of the former.

§2.2   *Illustrations of ontological functors*
§2.21   *Functors of inclusion*
§2.211   *Singular inclusion*

Form: $a \in b$
Truth-conditions: II.1 or II.3 only must represent the semantical status of '*a*' and '*b*'.

The nearest natural-language correlate of the '... ∈ ...' here in question may be found in languages which have no articles, e.g. Latin. Thus the Latin *est* of *Socrates est philosophus* 'Socrates is (a) philosopher' is a fair representation of the sense intended. In English we have 'is'-sentences such as 'Elizabeth is queen', but more usually 'a' or 'an' follow the 'is'. It should be noted that *any* two noun-expressions in the places of 'a' and 'b' give a well-formed expression. Thus the following, although all false, are nevertheless not ill-formed: 'Man ∈ mortal', 'Pegasus ∈ winged', 'Winged ∈ Pegasus', 'Pegasus ∈ Pegasus'. Alternatively, one may have the following specification (*LTD* 18): a proposition of the type 'a ∈ b' will be regarded as true if and only if the expression which stands in place of 'a' is an unshared noun-expression and if the only object designated by it happens to be designated by the noun-expression which stands in place of 'b'. The '... ∈ ...' here specified is the primitive term of the axiom first used for Ontology by Leśniewski (*LR* T34); this axiom will be used below, although as *LR* shows, it is not by any means the shortest, nor does it involve the only possible primitive term.

It will later be shown that there are indefinitely more senses of 'is', i.e. the material of the present paragraph should not be taken to entail the supposition that 'is' is univocal, and has only the sense here described (cf. §5.19).

§2.212   *Strong inclusion*

> Form: *a* ⊏ *b*
> Truth-conditions: II.1, II.3, II.9, and II.10 are in this case the only admissible alternative representations of the semantical status of 'a' and 'b'.

A reading convention which may be used for a natural language version of this functor is 'Every *a* is *b*'. Note that the truth of an expression of this form implies the existence of *a* and *b* (i.e. neither of these noun-expressions must be empty). A systematic definition is given at §4.3.4.

§2.213   *Weak inclusion*

> Form: *a* ⊂ *b*
> Truth-conditions: II.1, II.3, II.8, II.9, II.10, II.15, and II.16 are in this case the only admissible alternative representations of the semantical status of 'a' and 'b'.

A reading convention which may be used is 'All *a* is *b*', although in some contexts a more congruous expression may result from still retaining the 'Every *a* is *b*' reading suggested for strong inclusion (e.g. in III §4.18, .19). It is obvious from the alternatives listed above that if a given strong inclusion is true, then the corresponding weak inclusion is also true, but not *vice versa*, since there is no guarantee that the alternative which is fulfilled in respect of the case of the weak inclusion will be one which makes true the corresponding strong inclusion. A systematic definition is given at §4.3.5.

§2.214   *Partial inclusion*

> Form: $a \triangle b$
> Truth-conditions: II.1, II.3, II.4, II.9, II.10, II.11, and II.12 are in this case the only admissible alternative representations of the semantical status of '*a*' and '*b*'.

A reading convention which may be used is 'Some *a* is *b*'. For a systematic definition see §4.3.6. The alternatives listed here and in connection with the other forms of inclusion as truth-conditions permit the following listing of the 'if . . . then . . .' relations which hold between corresponding exemplifications of those various forms (i.e. exemplifications in which the names standing in place of '*a*' and '*b*' are constant from antecedent to consequent in respect of each of the following statements):

> If the *singular* is true, then the *strong* is true
> If the *singular* is true, then the *weak* is true
> If the *strong* is true, then the *weak* is true
> If the *singular* is true, then the *partial* is true
> If the *strong* is true, then the *partial* is true

But note that the following does *not* hold:

> If the *weak* is true, then the *partial* is true

The systematic definitions which are to be presented below will reflect these relations. One of the interesting results which may already be foreseen is the lack of any necessity for the breakdown which is sometimes alleged to occur in the 'immediate inferences' and 'square of opposition' of traditional logic, as well as in some modes of the syllogism; the narrowness of the conceptions leading to this 'breakdown' is avoided by the variety of inclusions suggested above.

§2.22   *Functors of identity*

§2.2201   The terminology hereunder suggested should be compared with that for inclusion, as certain obvious parallels are reflected in the titles of the two sets of functors.

§2.221   *Singular identity*

> Form: $a = b$
> Truth-conditions: in this case II.1 is the only admissible representation of the semantical status of '*a*' and '*b*'.

The reading convention '*a* is the same object as *b*' may be adopted. This type of identity is true, it may be noted, when '*a*' and '*b*' are unshared non-fictitious noun-expressions which designate the same object only. A systematic definition is given at §4.3.10.

§2.222   *Strong identity*

> Form: $a \,\square\, b$
> Truth-conditions: II.1 and II.9 are in this case the only alternative admissible representations of the semantical status of '*a*' and '*b*'.

The reading convention 'Only every *a* is *b*' may be adopted. From the alternatives mentioned it is plain that in the case of a true strong identity '*a*' and '*b*' may be shared or unshared noun-expressions. Further, if a singular identity is true, then the corresponding strong identity is also true (cf. §2.214). For a systematic definition see §4.3.11.

§2.223   *Weak identity*

> Form: $a \,\bigcirc\, b$
> Truth-conditions: II.1, II.9, and II.16 are in this case the only alternative admissible representations of the semantical status of '*a*' and '*b*'.

The reading convention 'Only all *a* is *b*' may be adopted. From the alternatives mentioned it is evident that a weak identity can be true even though both the noun-expressions involved are empty. In this it differs from the two types of identity previously described. A systematic definition is given at §4.3.12.

§2.224   Enough has already been said in this purely informal exposition to demonstrate the possibility of conceptions of identity such that there can be no single answer to the question, 'Does identity involve existence?'. From the forms of identity described in §2.221 and §2.222 it is clear that their truth allows one to infer the existence of *a* and *b* (§2.221) or of *a*'s and *b*'s (§2.222). No such inference can be envisaged from the weak identity described in §2.223. Hence, on the assumption that logical discourse is essentially neutral as regards existence—a *desideratum* which will be shown to be fulfillable in Ontology, but not in certain other systems—it is clear that while

.1 $[a] \,.\, a \bigcirc a$

(i.e., when '*a*' is a nominal variable, 'For all *a*—only all *a* is *a*') will turn out to be a thesis of logic, the corresponding expression in terms of singular identity

.2 $[a] \,.\, a = a$

(i.e. 'For all a—a is the same object as a') will not be a thesis. Nevertheless, some modern logicians are prepared to drop the existential neutrality of logic to the extent of admitting a sentence having the same effect as .2 as a logical thesis. This admission has its roots in a certain quantification theory, as will be shown in §2.25 below. The distinctions just proposed are also of service when one is construing Russell's discussion of identity in connection with the Theory of Descriptions (*RI* ch. XVI). It is, of course, plain that identities involving singular or strong forms of identity *can* become logical theses if they are prefaced by an existence statement as a hypothetical antecedent, thus:

.3 $[a]$. if there exists exactly one a, then $a = a$
.4 $[a]$. if there exists at least one a, then $a \square a$

(For more information on expressions such as the '$[a]$' here employed, see §2.25 below.)

§2.23   *Functors of existence*

§2.2301   The antecedent existence statements of the last two numbered expressions of the last paragraph already serve as a reminder of the need (which is fulfilled in Ontology) of having at our disposal means of asserting or denying existence which are not so closely entangled with the separate considerations of quantification as they are in the more familiar systems of logic (cf. §2.25). The functors whose preliminary informal outline is given below fulfil this need. Here, as in the case of §2.221, it is emphasised that the senses of existence suggested below are *not* put forward as being the only ones. Means will be provided later of extending the present senses of existence outwards in an unlimited range (§5.19). This will be one way of recognising that *being* is not univocal—a recognition which allows Ontology to avoid certain pitfalls to which those who, perhaps half-unconsciously, presuppose the univocity of being, are exposed.

§2.231   *First functor of existence*

Form: ex(a)
Truth-conditions: I.1 and I.2 are in this case the only alternative admissible representations of the semantical status of 'a'.

A reading convention which may be adopted is, 'There exists at least one a'. Statements of this form correspond to what in QDE are called 'general existence statements', since they are suitable for use (though not exclusively so) in those cases where 'a' is a shared name. See §4.3.1 for a systematic definition.

§2.232   *Second functor of existence*

> Form: sol(*a*)
> Truth-conditions: I.1 and I.3 are in this case the only
> alternative admissible representations of the semantical
> status of '*a*'.

A reading convention which may be adopted is 'There exists at most one *a*'. From the truth-conditions it is apparent that this functor is suitable (though not exclusively so) in those cases where '*a*' is an empty name. See §4.3.2 for a systematic definition.

§2.233   *Third functor of existence*

> Form: ob(*a*)
> Truth-conditions: I.1 is in this case the only admissible
> representation of the semantical status of '*a*'.

Reading conventions which may be adopted are 'There exists exactly one *a*', or '*a* is an object'. See §4.3.3 for a systematic definition of this functor. The second of the suggestions for reading this functor relies on the supposition that 'That of which there is exactly one' is acceptable as a most general description of what is involved in being an object. It is most important to realise that this most general conception is susceptible of specification in all manner of ways, not merely on Ontology, but in its extensions such as Mereology (Theory of part and whole), Chronology (Theory of time), or Stereology (Theory of space). In Ontology itself, however, it is already possible to specify an indefinitely large number of extensions of the sense of 'object' by reference to the various senses of '... is ...' of which §5.19 shows a first example. Finally it may be remarked that existence statements of the third form described above correspond to the 'singular existence statements' of *QDE*, since this third existence functor is suitable for use in those cases where '*a*' is an unshared name.

§2.24   The functors hitherto described are offered as samples of those which will be formally defined later (§4 below). All the points which have been made informally in connection with the various functors (e.g. their inferential interrelations) will be given systematic expression by means of the definitions which are to be proposed.

§2.25   *Quantification* (cf. *LLE*)

§2.2501   It is to be stressed that the remarks made hereunder by no means purport to constitute an exhaustive treatment of the topic of quantification. In accordance with the general policy of the present part, they merely offer a preliminary informal rendering of the situation sufficient for our limited purposes.

§2.251 *First supposition.* Let a universe consisting of only two objects be supposed, and let their unshared names be '*a*' and '*b*'; in terms of §2.233, therefore, 'ob(*a*)' and 'ob(*b*) are both true. Further, let '$\varphi(\quad)$' represent some proposition-forming functor which forms a proposition out of a single name; an example of such a functor would be '. . . moves'. In this situation one is immediately faced with two possibilities. First, both '$\varphi(a)$' and '$\varphi(b)$' may be true (e.g. '*a* moves' and '*b* moves' are both true). The realisation of this possibility can be represented by the form:

.1 $[x]\ \varphi(x)$

This may be read off as 'For all *x*, φ of *x*' (or as 'Each entity *x* is such that φ of *x*'); e.g. 'For all *x*, *x* moves'. Here '*x*' is a variable whose substituends are the unshared constant names '*a*' and '*b*'. It is clear that under the conditions of this first case, the expression .1 holds only when the following holds:

.2 $\varphi(a)$ and $\varphi(b)$

The second possibility is that either '$\varphi(a)$' or '$\varphi(b)$' are non-exclusively true. This possibility can be represented by the form:

.3 $[\exists x]\ \varphi(x)$

This may be read off as 'There exists an *x* such that φ of *x*'; e.g. 'There exists an *x* such that *x* moves'. Here '*x*' is, as in the first case, a variable covering the unshared constant names '*a*' and '*b*', but now .3 holds only when the following holds:

.4 $\varphi(a)$ or $\varphi(b)$

These 'definitions', under the convention that '*x*' is to be a variable whose possible substituends are the two names in question, are plainly laws for the two-object universe described. As we have seen, the expression '$[x]$' may under these circumstances be read off as 'For all *x*' (or as 'Each entity *x* is such that . . .'), and the expression '$[\exists x]$' may be read off as 'There exists an *x* such that . . .'. Alternatively the latter expression may also have 'For some *x* . . .' as its reading. Expressions of the first sort may be called 'universal' quantifiers, and those of the second sort 'existential' or 'particular' quantifiers.

§2.2511 *Extension of the first supposition.* As it is plainly desirable that the system should not make any presuppositions as to the number of objects in the universe, it might at first sight appear that one could retain the notation suggested in the last paragraph, and merely extend the range of the conjuncts (as shown in §2.251.2) and of the disjuncts (as shown in §2.251.4) to comprise any number of objects. However, in case there happened to be an infinity of objects, it would be impossible to enumerate them, even schematically, in the conjunctive or disjunctive components of the 'definitions' given above. In other words, those 'definitions' must be weakened in order that the possibility of the infinite case should not be disallowed. Retaining, therefore, the form shown at §2.251.1 as the universal ('for all x . . .') quantifier, and bearing in mind the fact that the truth of a conjunction of propositions (even though infinite) implies the truth of any one of its conjuncts, one can at least have the following as a law, when 'a' is an unshared name, no matter what the number of objects in the universe:

.1   If $[x]\ \varphi(x)$ then $\varphi(a)$

e.g. If for all x, x moves, then a moves. This weakening of the 'definition' yields what *QML* calls the 'rule of universal instantiation', i.e. that which is true in respect of all is true in respect of each. Similarly, retaining the form shown at §2.251.3 as the particular ('For some x . . .') or existential ('There exists an x such that . . .') quantifier, and bearing in mind the fact that the truth of one disjunct of a disjunction of propositions (even though that disjunction is infinite) implies the truth of the whole disjunction, one can at least have the following as a law, where 'a' is an unshared name, no matter what the number of objects in the universe:

.2   If $\varphi(a)$ then $[\exists x]\ \varphi(x)$

e.g. If a runs then for some x (*or* there exists an x such that) x runs. This weaking of the 'definition' yields what *QML* calls the 'rule of existential generalisation', i.e. that which is true of *one* is true of *some* (where 'some' means 'at least one').

§2.2512   The first supposition which has now been outlined represents (with one important reservation to be mentioned in §2.2525) the common interpretation of nominal quantifiers in current logic. However, it has the disadvantage of causing the quantifier '$[\exists x]$' to run together two notions which can in principle be seen as separable. First of all there is the notion of what may be called 'somehood', as reflected in its 'for some x . . .' reading, and as opposed to the 'allhood' covered by the universal quantifier. Secondly, there is the notion of existence which is reflected in its other possible reading as 'There exists an x such that . . .'. The results of this running together are quite extensive and undesirable, and its disadvantages in the field of the analysis of medieval logic may well be imagined; see, for example, III §4. The question hence arises: Is there any way in which this confusion may be avoided? This question may be answered in terms of the second supposition, which now follows.

§2.252 *Second supposition.* Let the same universe as that of the first supposition be posited, i.e. let there be two objects only, whose proper names are '*a*' and '*b*'. But now, in addition, suppose a fictitious name '*c*' (i.e. it is not the case that ex(*c*), to use the functor proposed at §2.231) and a shared name '*d*' which names both object *a* and object *b*. Any further noun expression would be synonymous with one or other of '*a*', '*b*', '*c*', or '*d*'. Now we can, on the same lines as before (§2.251), determine the senses of '[*x*]' and '[∃*x*]', but with '*x*' as a variable whose substituends may be drawn from *all* the sorts of names previously described (§1.3) and which are now at our disposal (i.e. shared, unshared, fictitious), and not merely from the unshared names of the first supposition. Thus the situation is now as follows:

.1A $[x] \, \varphi(x)$

holds only if the following also holds:

.1B $\varphi(a)$ and $\varphi(b)$ and $\varphi(c)$ and $\varphi(d)$

Similarly

.2A $[\exists x] \, \varphi(x)$

holds only if the following also holds:

.2B $\varphi(a)$ or $\varphi(b)$ or $\varphi(c)$ or $\varphi(d)$

Here .1A and .1B represent the 'for all *x*' conception and .2A and .2B the 'for some *x*' conception in the two-object universe.

§2.2521 *Extension of the second supposition.* This second supposition may now be extended in exactly the same manner as was the first in §2.2511, and with exactly the same preliminary results, i.e. §2.2511.1 ('rule of universal instantiation') and §2.2511.2 ('rule of existential generalisation') still hold in the now possibly many-object universe, but it is now plain that the latter title for §2.2511.2 will not do. It is now no longer proper to read off '[∃*x*]' as 'There exists an *x* such that . . .' since the antecedent chosen for the form shown at §2.2511.2 might be '$\varphi(c)$'; the rule §2.2511.2 still then holds, but it is essential in this case (and hence in any case) that the consequent should be read off as, 'For some *x*, $\varphi(x)$' only, since faced with the possibility of the use of the empty name '*c*' in the antecedent, one cannot safely extract an existential statement in the consequent. In this way, the *desideratum* suggested above (§2.2512) has been attained: 'somehood' has been concentrated in the quantifier, and *only* 'somehood'; existence (as distinct from 'somehood') can be separately and overtly expressed elsewhere in quantified sentences. It is for this purpose that the various functors of existence sketched above will be exploited, thereby abolishing certain confusions which vitiate some contemporary logic, and at the same time unfit it for the analysis of medieval logical theses.

§2.2521   As a preliminary indication of the sort of difficulty to which the first supposition (§2.251) gives rise, let us consider the consequences of *QML*'s acceptance of the 'rule of existential generalisation' (§2.2511.2). The symbol 'φ' of the antecedent of that rule is designed to call attention to what may be called *predicates*, i.e. functors which, when completed by their single argument which is a name, form a proposition. Now 'exists' is such a functor, and so is 'does not exist'. If now the 'a' of that antecedent is 'Pegasus' and the 'φ' is 'does not exist', then that antecedent represents the true proposition 'Pegasus does not exist'. But the rule then commits one to the inference of 'There exists an x such that x does not exist' (given the 'existential' reading off of the quantifier which goes with the first supposition) and this is plainly a contradiction. There are, of course, various ways out of this difficulty: one can either deny that 'Pegasus' is a name, or deny that 'does not exist' is a predicate, or both. Alternatively, one may even go so far as to deny that sentences such as 'Pegasus exists', 'Socrates exists', 'Pegasus does not exist', 'Socrates does not exist' make sense at all, if 'Pegasus' and 'Socrates' are construed as names; such are, in fact, the common or garden expedients in these circumstances. In the first case one goes against one's unperverted pre-philosophical convictions; until the difficulty had arisen, would it have been *obvious* that 'Pegasus' is not a name? St Anselm of Canterbury has, after all, an excellent discussion on the way in which empty names have meaning (III §4, cf. *HL* §6.6). In the second case one is placing an unfortunate restriction on the generality of one's logic. There is no question that a predicate can be defined in the way suggested above; this will be agreed on all hands. Yet suddenly, because of an easily-avoidable hitch arising from notation, one finds that a restriction must be placed on the generality of that definition. Clearly, if it is possible to retain that generality (as is in fact possible in terms of the second supposition, with its separation of 'somehood' and existence) then that retention is preferable. Again, a consequence of denying that 'does not exist' is a predicate is that 'exists' is not a predicate either, so that one is faced with the startling news that 'Socrates exists' is nonsense or even worse than nonsense (*RI* 164).

Now while it is perfectly true that it is philosophically most important to realise that the grammatical form of a sentence need not be its true logical form, lightly-made claims as to the discrepancy between the two, or accusations of nonsensicalness in what has hitherto been perfectly respectable ordinary discourse, should not be lightly propounded. The reason is plain: the incapacity of a logical system to adapt itself to pretheoretical manners of utterance may well arise from lack of flexibility in the system in terms of which those utterances are being measured, rather than from some logical defect in the utterances themselves. This lack of flexibility bodes ill for any attempt to apply such systems to the analysis of medieval logical utterances (cf. *HL* §6.6). Essay I of *QF* may be consulted as an excellent exposition of the difficulties described above as arising from something like the first supposition and its extension; it there becomes apparent that such quantification leaves us with no *prima facie* means of saying that something does not exist. As a consequence one is forced into accepting the Theory of Definite Descriptions (a theory of what Abelard called 'proper verbs') as an expedient to resolve an awkward situation. The Theory of Descriptions is, within its limits, most respectable; the manner in which it has to be brought to bear, in the form of an *ad hoc* expedient, in order that the system can continue to be adequate, is not.

§2.2522   Under the terms of the second supposition and its extension, however, the difficulties described do not arise. What was previously known as the 'rule of existential generalisation' (§2.2511.2) can now be used in all its generality, without restrictions, and without the necessity of having to check, in a way foreign to logic, that a given name is non-empty. One *can* now have 'Pegasus' as the '*a*' of the antecedent and 'does not exist' as the case of '*φ*'. The conclusion which the rule allows one to draw, namely: 'For some *x*, *x* does not exist' makes perfect sense, is true, and is provable (§5.37) thanks to the admission of empty names. It is now no longer *necessary* to re-parse all sentences of the form which has been under consideration in case the names involved should happen to be empty. Neither is it necessary to adhere to the *dictum* that existence 'is not a predicate'. Of course, such re-parsing is still *possible* in Ontology, and it may well turn out that existence-predicates differ from others in all sorts of ways. This moderate, unparadoxical thesis at the same time allows substitutions for predicate-variables to be undertaken without any restrictions as to the range of those substitutions.

§2.2523   The nature of the material of the previous paragraphs is sufficient to make it clear that the adoption of the following nomenclature is not unjustified: let us call that type of quantification which proceeds in the manner of the first supposition and its extension *restricted* quantification, and that which proceeds in the manner of the second supposition and its extension *unrestricted* quantification. The latter will be adopted in this present work. Lest its adoption should appear to give rise to an unwarranted and inconvenient separation from the main body of current logical-philosophical work which revolves round the restricted quantification it is pointed out that the rule for translating expressions using the restricted interpretation into expressions using the unrestricted interpretation is quite simple: expressions of the type '$[x]\, \varphi(x)$' and '$[\exists x]\, \varphi(x)$' become expressions of the types '$[x]$ if x exists then $\varphi(x)$' and '$[\exists x]\, x$ exists and φx' respectively. Other expressions remain unchanged. (The 'x exists' of the translation will, of course, be rendered in terms of an appropriate functor of existence; see §2.23.) The main practical point is that the quantifier '$[\exists \dots]$' which is usually read off as 'There exists ... such that ...' should now be rendered exclusively as 'For some...'. In keeping with this position, the terms 'existential quantification' and 'existential quantifier' no longer have application: 'particular quantification' and 'particular quantifier' are now respectively the more apt titles. What has hitherto been referred to as the 'rule of existential generalisation' correspondingly becomes the 'rule of particular generalisation'.

§2.2524   In order to make clear the reasons for the adoption of the title 'restricted quantification', let a parallel case be considered; this will illuminate the manner in which adoption of such quantification robs its users of the power of saying certain things. Suppose a language in which the names substitutable for the nominal variables are restricted to the proper names of human beings. In the resulting language, the following would be true:

.1 $[x]\, x$ is a human being

This corresponds to the necessity of accepting the following in systems using restricted quantification:

.2 $[x]\, x$ exists

Again, in the language supposed one could *not* assert

.3 $[\exists x]\, x$ is not a human being

This corresponds to the trouble encountered in systems employing restricted quantification in asserting the non-existence of named objects, i.e. the impossibility of saying

.4 $[\exists x]\, x$ does not exist

Thanks, however, to the dissociation of 'somehood' from existence which operates in the unrestricted quantification of Ontology, the restrictions can be made quite explicit. The startling news that everything exists (.2 above) really amounts to

.5   For all x in respect of which $\mathrm{ob}(x)$, $\mathrm{ex}(x)$

which, from the Ontological Table alone may be seen to be obviously true. Indeed, the following restatement of .2 and .5 in terms of unrestricted quantification and the functors of existence will be demonstrated at §5.2 below:

.6   [x] if ob(x) then ex(x)

Again, the impossibility of asserting, in a language employing restricted quantification, that

.7   [∃x] x does not exist

really amounts to a reminder of the falsehood of

.8   For some x in respect of which ob(x), it is not the case that ex(x)

i.e., in unrestricted terms:

.9   [∃x] ob(x) and it is not the case that ex(x)

This is clearly false, as the Ontological Table alone suffices to show.

§2.2525   Finally we come to the reservation mentioned in §2.2512: this reservation was as to the exactitude of the first supposition and its extensions in representing restricted quantificational doctrine. Throughout the foregoing discussion quantifiers and variables have been explained in terms of *expressions* (e.g. names) as opposed to the circumstances or things signified by (e.g. named by) those expressions. In point of fact restricted quantification is usually explained by saying that the *range* of that sort of quantification lies in the *things named* by the substituends for the variables. In the foregoing discussion substituends rather than objects were made the focal point or the explanation. This focal point was adopted because of the fact that it is more convenient to explain unrestricted quantification in terms of expressions (substituends). This should not be taken to entail that the *range* of unrestricted quantification consists of expressions. It by no means follows from the method of explanation adopted above that sentences involving unrestricted quantification are metalinguistic sentences, i.e. sentences having expressions only, rather than things other than expressions, as the range of their quantifiers.

§3   PUNCTUATION

§3.1   The following Peano–Russell style of symbolism for functors which form propositions from propositions will be used for the account of Ontology which is now to be given:

> '*p . q*' for '*p* and *q*'
> '*p* ∨ *q*' for '*p* or *q*'
> '*p* ⊃ *q*' for 'if *p* then *q*'
> '*p* ≡ *q*' for '*p* if and only if *q*'
> '~*p*' for 'it is not the case that *p*'

Now punctuation is necessary in connection with this symbolism, and is in many respects similar to that of common algebra. In the latter, phrasing can be shown by parentheses, thus:

.1 $a \times (b + c)$
.2 $(a \times b) + c$

If now the convention is adopted that the scope of a parenthesis extends away from the functor which it adjoins, then it becomes possible to use only one-sided parenthetic symbols. Thus the expression shown below in .3 could be equally well represented as in .4:

.3 $\{[a \times (b + c)] \times d\} = \{(f \times g) + h\}$
.4 $a \times (b + c] \times d\} = \{f \times g) + h$

It is of course understood that in .4 the scope of the 'weaker' (lower-order) parenthesis is terminated when it encounters a 'stronger' (higher-order) parenthesis. The same idea may now be carried into the field of logical punctuation, using one dot where the weakest one-sided parenthesis is appropriate, two dots where a one-sided parenthesis a degree stronger than the first is to be indicated, and so on. As an example consider the case in which an identical set of symbols is punctuated in two ways. Let it first be punctuated thus:

.5 $[(p \equiv q) \vee r] \supset (s \vee t)$

With one-sided parentheses this becomes:

.6 $p \equiv q) \vee r] \supset (s \vee t$

And finally, replacing these one-sided parentheses with corresponding numbers of dots, one has:

.7 $p \equiv q \,.\, \vee r : \supset .\, s \vee t$

The same symbols as occur in .5 (with the exception of the now rearranged brackets) are used in .8 which now follows. It is accompanied by .9 and .10 which further illustrate the moves *via* the one-sided parentheses to the dotted version (.10):

.8 $\{[p \equiv (q \vee r)] \supset s\} \vee t$
.9 $p \equiv (q \vee r] \supset s\} \vee t$
.10 $p \equiv .\, q \vee r : \supset s : .\, \vee t$

To this simple scheme must be added further complications in order to take account of the facts that in the notation to be used a dot ('.') already represents a conjunction, and that quantifiers are usually found at the beginning of sentences of Ontology. Theoretically the complications need not be introduced. One could, at a pinch, place dots on either side of a conjunction dot, but the additional conventions now to be mentioned allow a dot or group of dots to function both as a conjunction and as punctuation, thereby making for economy. It is, of course, perfectly plain when dots are being used as the sign of conjunction, since they are then flanked on both sides by propositional expressions. And again, the scope of dots immediately following a quantifier plainly should not (unlike what holds in the case of conjunction dots) extend in *both* directions, but only to the right of that quantifier.

§3.2   The complications mentioned may be expressed as follows: given the *general* rule that the scope of a dot or group of dots extends outwards from the functor which it adjoins, or in the case of a dot or group of dots representing 'and', in both directions, or in the case of a dot or dots immediately following a quantifier, to the right, and that that scope extends to the point where a greater number of dots occurs (or, should no such encounter occur, that scope extends to the end or ends of the expressions), one may add the conventions:

(i) The scope of dots immediately adjoining a functor is *never stopped by an equal number* of dots ('Dots immediately adjoining a functor' is not here taken to imply reference to dots representing a conjunction, in respect of which see (iii)).

(ii) The scope of dots immediately following a quantifier is *sometimes stopped by an equal number* of dots, i.e. only when those dots immediately adjoin a functor. Hence that scope extends over an equal number of dots which represent a conjunction, or which immediately follow upon another quantifier.

(iii) The scope of dots which represent the conjunction 'and' is *always stopped by an equal number* of dots, whatever the position of occurrence of the latter.

The italicised 'never—sometimes—always' expression of these conventions, as in (i) to (iii) above, makes them easily memorisable, and may be illustrated by reference to a sentence of Ontology, thus:

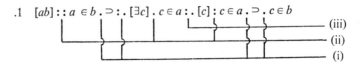

.1 $[ab]::a \in b . \supset : . [\exists c] . c \in a : . [c] : c \in a . \supset . c \in b$

Here the conventions which apply to each dot or set of dots in the expression are indicated by the Roman numeral on the right.

§3.2   This is also a suitable point at which to add that when expressions which consist of more than a single propositional variable are negated they are placed in parentheses, and the expression thus formed is then prefaced by the sign of propositional negation. Thus the negation of '$a \in b$' will be expressed as:

.1 $\sim (a \in b)$

i.e. 'It is not the case that $a \in b$'.

§4   DEFINITIONS

§4.1   The nature of certain functors which occur in Ontology has already been informally outlined with the help of the table given in §2.2. These and other functors will now be brought into the scope of a system by the use of one of them, namely '$\in$', as a primitive functor in terms of which the rest may be defined. There is no necessity that this should be the primitive functor, as *LR* well demonstrates. As, however, the aim is to expound that minimum of Ontology which will suffice for the elucidations of samples of medieval themes, the use of alternative primitive terms for the purpose of definition and axiomatisation will not be discussed here.

§4.2   Leśniewski's contention was that the rules in terms of which definitions are carried out should be very carefully stated. Once stated, they constitute a sort of challenge to the reader to use those same rules and see whether or not they allow undesirable absurdities to be imported into the system. In systems other than those of Leśniewski, rules of definition are scarcely ever made explicit, and the reader is hence (one must assume) left free to gather the rules from the practice; since any one practice can be carried out in terms of many sets of rules, there is under these circumstances no guarantee that the reader may not interpret the practice in a way not intended by the author, and in the light of such interpretation introduce undesirable elements into extensions of the system. As a full statement of rules of definition can be exceedingly complex, it will suffice for the purposes of the present exposition merely to state that definitions are theses of the system (and not mere 'typographical conveniences' or 'abbreviations') which introduce new terms not having previously occurred in the system. Strictly speaking therefore, the definitions should follow and not precede the axiom which will later be given.

Definitions may be of at least two sorts, namely *Protothetical* and *Ontological*. The first sort, as the name implies, define functors which are ultimately propositional in nature, i.e. are suitable arguments for functors primarily characteristic of Protothetic. The definitional frame used in such cases may be depicted as follows:

.1 $[\ldots] . \alpha \equiv \beta$

4

Here 'α' is the *definiendum* which is defined by the *definiens* 'β', the latter making use of terms which have already occurred in the system (including the primitive term which figures in the axiom adopted); see *LR* 172–3. The second sort, the *Ontological*, define names or name-like expressions or functors which ultimately form such expressions and are hence suitable as arguments of those functors which are most characteristic of Ontology, i.e. functors which form propositions from names. In this case the definitional frame may have the form:

.2 $[a \ldots] : a \in \Psi . \equiv . a \in a . \varphi(a)$

wherein 'Ψ' is *not* a predicate variable, but a dummy symbol for a constant name or a nominal function. '$\varphi(a)$' stands for a propositional expression in which 'a' occurs; *LR* 173–4, *LCM* 322–3. The nature and intention of this last definitional frame are perfectly transparent: in order to introduce something as a so-and-so (where the name 'so-and-so' is unfamiliar to the hearer or reader) it is only necessary to point out that a is a so-and-so if and only if a exists and the conditions for being a so-and-so (specified in the 'φ' of .2) hold of a. Both the right-hand clauses of .2 are clearly indispensable. In spite of its simplicity and obviousness (or perhaps because of these) this definitional frame will play a weighty part in obviating a form of Russell's paradox (see §5 below).

§4.3   Now follow some Protothetical definitions in which the '$\in$' of §2.211 is assumed as primitive term; several of the functors here defined have already been informally described in terms of the table given at §2.12. The suggestions for reading the functors in English *are* only suggestions, and do *not* carry with them the implication that the accompanying definitions give the only possible analyses of the respective English versions.

.1 $[a] : \mathrm{ex}(a) . \equiv . [\exists b] . b \in a$ (*LR* T1)
         (First functor of existence. Read 'There exists at least one
         a'; cf. §2.231)

.2 $[a] : . \mathrm{sol}(a) . \equiv : [bc] : b \in a . c \in a . \supset . b \in c$ (*LR* T5)
         (Second functor of existence. Read 'There exists at most
         one a'; cf. §2.232)

.3 $[a] : \mathrm{ob}(a) . \equiv . [\exists b] . a \in b$ (*LR* T16)
         (Third functor of existence. Read 'There exists exactly one
         a'; cf. §2.233)

.4 $[ab] : : a \sqsubset b . \equiv : . [\exists c] . c \in a : . [c] : c \in a . \supset . c \in b$
                                                                                                            (*LR* T18)

         (Strong inclusion. Read 'Every a is b'; cf. §2.212)

.5 $[ab] :. a \subset b . \equiv : [c] : c \in a . \supset . c \in b$

(Weak inclusion. Read 'All a is b'; cf. §2.213)   (*LR* T19)

.6 $[ab] : a \triangle b . \equiv . [\exists c] . c \in a . c \in b$ (*LR* T20)

(Partial inclusion. Read 'Some a is b'; cf. §2.214)

.7 $[ab] :: a \sqsubset\!\!\!\top b . \equiv :. [\exists c] . c \in a :. [c] : c \in a . \supset . \sim (c \in b)$

(*LR* T22)

(Strong exclusion. Read 'Every a is-not b')

.8 $[ab] :. a \not\subset b . \equiv : [c] : c \in a . \supset . \sim (c \in b)$ (*LR* T23)

(Weak exclusion. Read 'No a is b')

.9 $[ab] : a \triangle\!\!\!\backslash b . \equiv . [\exists c] . c \in a . \sim (c \in b)$ (*LR* T24)

(Partial exclusion. Read 'Some a is-not b')

.10 $[ab] : a = b . \equiv . a \in b . b \in a$ (*LR* T25)

(Singular identity. Read 'a is the same object as b'; cf. §2.221)

.11 $[ab] :: a \square b . \equiv :. [\exists c] . c \in a :. [c] : c \in a . \equiv . c \in b$

(*LR* T26)

(Strong identity. Read 'Only every a is b'; cf. §2.222)

.12 $[ab] :. a \bigcirc b . \equiv : [c] : c \in a . \equiv . c \in b$ (*LR* T27)

(Weak identity. Read 'Only all a is b'; cf. §2.223)

Now follow some Ontological definitions:

.13 $[a] : a \in \vee . \equiv . a \in a$ (*LR* T72)

(The '$\vee$' here defined may be read off as 'object' or 'existing object')

.14 $[a] : a \in \wedge . \equiv . a \in a . \sim (a \in a)$ (*LR* T73)

(The '$\wedge$' here defined may be read off as 'object which does not exist')

.15 $[a] : a \,\aleph\, (b) . \equiv . a \in a . \sim (a \in b)$ (*LT* T74)

(The '$\aleph(\ )$' here defined may be read off as 'non- . . . .')

Definitions .13 and .14 provide, among other things, nominal senses of 'some thing' and 'no thing', in the absence of which analyses of certain medieval puzzles about being and nothingness would be impossible (see, for instance, III §4 and *HL* §6.6). Definition .15 covers what could be called 'nominal' negation as opposed to the more familiar propositional negation ('$\sim$'). This distinction was something quite familiar to ancient and medieval logicians, as ch. 10 of Aristotle's *De Interpretatione*, Aquinas' commentary thereon (*APH* 213, 217), as well as Boethius' commentary (*B* 344–8, esp. 365B, 346B) all testify. However, contemporary logicians, for reasons connected with the symbolism which they choose to use at the outset of their expositions have lost sight of this simple and obvious distinction, with results that reach deep into their systems (cf. III §4). As an example of the way in which failure or notational incapacity to observe this distinction impinges on current logic, consider first of all that

.16 $[ab] : a \in b \,.\, \vee \,.\, \sim (a \in b)$

is a correct statement of an exemplification or particular case of the Principle of the Excluded Middle, i.e. $[p] \,.\, p \vee \sim p$. Note, however, that

.17 $[ab] : a \in b \,.\, \vee \,.\, a \in \mathsf{N} \,(b)$

is *not* a correct exemplification of that Principle, notwithstanding the fact that many contemporary logicians are prepared to assume that it is. One obvious reason for the unacceptability of .17 is the change from propositional negation (which occurs in the general principle) to nominal negation (which occurs in .17). In the absence of a justificatory rule, this shift may already be queried. A further reason for its unacceptability is because from '$a \in b$' one can infer '$[\exists b] \,.\, a \in b$' and from '$a \in \mathsf{N} \,(b)$' one can infer '$[\exists c] \,.\, a \in c$'. It therefore follows from .17 that

.18 $[a] : [\exists b] \,.\, a \in b \,.\, \vee \,.\, [\exists c] \,.\, a \in c$

Whence, by §4.3.3, one has:

.19 $[a] \,.\, \mathrm{ob}(a) \vee \mathrm{ob}(a)$

This, by the use of the thesis '$[p] : p \vee p \,.\, \supset \,.\, p$', yields

.20 $[a] \,.\, \mathrm{ob(a)}$

i.e. the 'everything exists' previously encountered in the discussion of quantification (§2.2524) and which is unacceptable to an existentially neutral logic such as Ontology. Nevertheless, systems employing restricted quantification are committed to .20, and this explains why proponents of such systems can easily afford to slur over the distinction between the two sorts of negation and hence accept .17 as a thesis. However, the necessity for making exactly the distinction in question catches up with them at certain crucial points (cf. III §4).

§5   AXIOM AND DEDUCTIONS

Some further definitions still remain to be stated. However, in the meantime, so as to illustrate the way in which those already brought forward may be immediately taken into action, here is Leśniewski's original (1920) axiom for Ontology, in the light of which deductions can be made:

.1 $[ab] :: a \in b . \equiv :. [\exists c] . c \in a :. [c] : c \in a . \supset . c \in b :.$
$[cd] : c \in a . d \in a . \supset . c \in d$

Formidable though it may appear at first sight, the import of this axiom is perfectly self-evident, as an elucidation given at .9 below will show. Strictly speaking, the definitions previously introduced for example's sake should now be restated, but in the present initiatory context such repetition may be eschewed.

Under these circumstances, given this axiom and such definitions as may be relevant, all of which are theses of the system, one can proceed to give proofs of further theses. The following is a first example:

.2 $[a] : ob(a) . \supset . ex(a)$
$[a] :.$
(1) $ob(a) . \supset :$		
(2) $[\exists b] . a \in b :$	(§4.3.3,	1)
(3) $[\exists c] . c \in a :$	(§5.1,	2)
$ex(a)$	(§4.3.1,	3)

Here the thesis to be proved is first stated, immediately following its reference number. It will be noted that this thesis is implicational in form, i.e. is an 'if . . . then . . .' proposition. Now clearly one should first write down the antecedent of the implication to be proved (numbered (1)) in order to check which expressions may justifiably stand as its consequent in an 'if . . . then . . .' ('. . . $\supset$ . . .') proposition, given the axiom and definitions at our disposal. We in fact discover that on the basis of §4.3.3 and (1) we may have the expression shown in line (2) as such a consequent. Further, on the basis of the axiom (§5.1) and line (2) we may have line (3). Finally, using the material now available in line (3), one can by the application of §4.3.1 pass from it to the desired consequent of the thesis to be proved, i.e. the 'ex(a)' of the final (unnumbered) line.

Other remarks on this simple technique of proof will be made below. Here now are some further proofs:

.3 $[a] : ob(a) . \supset . sol(a)$
$[a] ::$
(1) $ob(a) . \supset :.$		
(2) $[\exists b] . a \in b :.$	(§4.3.3,	1)
(3) $[cd] : c \in a . d \in a . \supset . c \in d :.$	(§5.1,	2)
$sol(a)$	(§4.3.2,	3)

.4 $[ab] :. a \in b . \supset : [c] : c \in a . \supset . c \in b$ (§5.1)

This last thesis can plainly be inferred from §5.1, which is here shown as its justification, in view of the propositional thesis $[p] : . p \equiv . q . r : \supset . p \supset r$. The intuitive acceptability of the steps made in such proofs is such that it would only complicate matters unnecessarily were the propositional thesis to which reference could be made invariably stated. No such statement need hence be made, except perhaps as a remark in exceptionally complex cases.

.5 $[abc] : a \in b . c \in a . \supset . c \in b$
          $[abc] : :$
            (1) $a \in b .$
            (2) $c \in a . \supset : .$
            (3) $[d] : d \in a . \supset . d \in b : .$ (§5.4,   1)
                $c \in b$ (3, 2)

This last example illustrates how, when the antecedent of the thesis to be proved consists of several conjuncts, each of them is stated as a separate assumption in the first lines of the proof.

.6 $[ab] : : b \in a : . [cd] : c \in a . d \in a . \supset . c \in d : . \supset . a \in b$
          $[ab] : :$
            (1) $b \in a : .$
            (2) $[cd] : c \in a . d \in a . \supset . c \in d : . \supset .$
            (3) $a \in a .$ (§5.1,   1, 2)
                $a \in b$ (2, 3, 1)

Some commentary may be helpful here. First of all, as regards the final step, whereby '$a \in b$' is derived on the grounds of (2), (3), and (1): (2) is in fact here used as a principle (it holds for *all* values of 'c' and 'd'). It therefore holds for the substitutions c/a, d/b (i.e. 'a' for 'c' and 'b' for 'd'), so that we have:

.601 $a \in a . b \in a . \supset . a \in b$

But the first clause of the antecedent of .601 is given by (3), the second by (1), and so we can hence pass to the consequent shown, i.e. '$a \in b$'. Secondly, as regards the penultimate step, whereby '$a \in a$' is derived in the light of §5.1 and (1) and (2): a little consideration will show that one in effect has at one's disposal, given (1) and (2), the whole of the right-hand side of the axiom §5.1, but with the substitution b/a. This is because (1) gives the first clause of that right-hand side (if $b \in a$, then clearly $[\exists c] . c \in a$), (2) is precisely the third conjunct of that right-hand side, and the remaining conjunct, in terms of the substitution mentioned, becomes an instance of the propositional thesis '$[p] . p \supset p$', i.e. '$[c] . c \in a . \supset . c \in a$', and hence is available to us. From this right-hand side of §5.1 (with the substitution b/a) the

left-hand side is clearly inferrable, but with the same substitution, i.e.
$a \in a$.

.7 $[a] : ex(a) . sol(a) . \supset .ob(a)$
       $[a] :: $
         (1) $ex(a) .$
         (2) $sol(a) . \supset : .$
         (3) $[bc] : b \in a . c \in a . \supset . b \in c : .$ (§4.3.2, 2)
           $[\exists b] .$
         (4) $b \in a .$ (§4.1.1, 1)
         (5) $a \in b : .$ (§5.6, 4, 3)
           $ob(a)$ (§4.4.3, 5)

Only the derivation of (5) perhaps here calls for a remark: (4) and
(3) together, to which appeal is there made, in fact amount to the
antecedent of §5.6, but with the substitutions c/b, d/c effected. Hence
the consequent of §5.6, i.e. $a \in b$, may be inferred.

.8 $[ab] : ob(a) . \equiv . ex(a) . sol(a)$ (.2, .3, and .7 of §5)
.9 $[ab] : a \in b . \equiv . ex(a) . a \subset b . sol(a)$
                                   (§5.1, and .1, .2, .5 of §4.3)

This last thesis is an elucidation of the axiom in terms of definitions
previously given.

    Further theses which will prove to be of interest (e.g. in relation
to III §5) are as follows:

.10 $[ab] : a = b . \supset . a \bigcirc b$
       $[ab] :: $
         (1) $a = b . \supset : .$
         (2) $a \in b .$ }   (§4.3.10, 1)
         (3) $b \in a : .$
         (4) $[c] : c \in a . \supset . c \in b : .$ (§5.1, 2)
         (5) $[c] : c \in b . \supset . c \in a : .$ (§5.1, 3)
           $a \bigcirc b$ (§4.3.12, 4, 5)
.11 $[ab] : a = b . \supset . ob(a)$
       $[ab] : $
         (1) $a = b . \supset .$
         (2) $a \in b .$ (§4.3.10, 1)
           $ob(a)$ (§4.3.3, 2)
.12 $[ab] : a = b . \supset . ob(b)$
       $[ab] : $
         (1) $a = b . \supset .$
         (2) $b \in a .$ (§4.3.10, 1)
           $ob(b)$ (§4.3.3, 2)
.13 $[a] : a \in a . \supset . a = a$ (§4.3.10)

Note that '$[a] . a = a$' is *not* a thesis, whereas the following is:

.14 $[a] . a \bigcirc a$ (§4.3.12, from $[p] . p \equiv p$)

Now comes yet another example of an Ontological definition:

.15 $[a\varphi] : a \in \text{trm}\langle\varphi\rangle . \equiv . a \in a . \varphi(a)$

Here a name-like expression 'trm$\langle\varphi\rangle$' is formed from the verb
(predicate) 'φ'; thus if 'φ' is 'leads', then 'trm$\langle\varphi\rangle$' is 'leader'.
Similarly, one can form 'writer' from 'write', 'killer' from 'kill',
'teacher' from 'teach', and so on. One may read 'trm$\langle\varphi\rangle$' as 'term
satisfying φ' or as 'φ-er' (cf. the use of the '-er' termination at I §3.1).

The last definition gave us 'trm$\langle \quad \rangle$' as a functor whereby a name
('trm$\langle\varphi\rangle$') is formed from a proposition-forming functor ('φ') which
takes one name as its argument. The reverse process, i.e. the formation
of verbs from names, as at I §3.2, can be performed in various ways,
one of which is exploited in the following definition:

.16 $[ab] : \in[\![b]\!] (a) . \equiv . a \in b$

Thus if 'b' is the name 'deputy', then '$\in[\![b]\!]$' is the verb 'deputises';
if 'b' is *rex*, then '$\in[\![b]\!]$' is *regnat*, and so on. In this case a verb (a
proposition-forming functor) having one name as its argument, is
formed from a name. This definition is the first of a series which
introduce 'many-link functors' of complex and often novel semantical
categories. Thus, assuming *name* and *verb* (or predicate) as basic
semantical categories, it is possible to build up an indefinitely large
number of new parts of speech of increasing complexity by means
of definitions introducing such many-link functors. Hence is fulfilled
the second of the *desiderata* mentioned at I §2 as essential if modern
logic is to come to terms with medieval. Definition .16 systematically
covers instances such as the derivation of the verb 'Pegasises' from
the noun 'Pegasus' (*QF* 8). Of course natural language does not
always display the universal verb–noun correlation which .15 and .16
guarantee for the language of Ontology. The 'barbaric' Latin of
medieval philosophers and logicians, comprising that proliferation of
abstract names against which Locke inveighs in *LE* III, was all part
of an attempt to obtain a similar guarantee by modifying a natural
language according to artificial rules.

Two other functors of the same semantical category as '$\in[\![\quad]\!]$' may
also be defined:

.17 $[ab] : \subset[\![a]\!] (b) . \equiv . b \subset a$
.18 $[ab] : \text{Cl}[\![a]\!] (b) . \equiv . b \bigcirc a$

The '$\subset[\![a]\!]$' might be rendered '. . . form an aggregate of a's', and
'Cl$[\![a]\!]$' as '. . . form the class of a's', both of which are plainly verbs

(predicates). According to context, some one or other of .16, .17, and .18 may correspond to the provisional '( )ise' verb-form of I §3.2.

Now verbs (predicates), including those which have just been defined, may themselves be arguments of an 'is', as in the medieval examples which are of the sort to which 'To walk is to move' belongs (*APH* 56, 96, 54, 55). Hence a proposition-forming functor which takes two such verbs as arguments must be envisaged; such a functor, although typographically and phonetically indistinguishable in pre-theoretical language from the 'is' which like '∈' has two nominal arguments, is nevertheless of a semantical category diverse from that of '∈'. This diversity should, in our notation, be marked by a difference of bracketing, as suggested in I §3, after the manner of the novel brackets already introduced in some of the foregoing definitions. For our present purposes it will, however, suffice to retain the '∈' as before and to allow the diversity of semantical category in this and kindred cases to be made apparent by the diversity of argument-signs. Only in III §5 will it become necessary to reintroduce distinguishing brackets. The higher-order 'is' ('∈') which takes verbs as arguments (cf. I §3.4) may be defined as follows:

.19 $[\varphi\psi] :: \varphi \in \psi . \equiv : . [\exists a] . \varphi(a) . \psi(a) : . [bc] : \varphi(b) . \varphi(c) .$
           $\supset . b \bigcirc c$

This definition yields for verbs the effect which the lower-order (nominal-argument) '∈' has in respect of names, and from it can be proved the higher-order analogue of the axiom .1.

Further subtle variations can be introduced by varying the sort of functor of identity which figures in the final (right-hand) clause of definition .19. In fact, the perspectives which this higher-order 'is' opens up are so numerous that only a selection of its possibilities can be mentioned here. For instance, the process exemplified in .19, whereby one makes available an 'is' which is one order higher than the primitive 'is' of Ontology, can in fact be prolonged indefinitely 'upwards' so to speak. Thus .19 itself can be the basis of yet a further '∈' which takes as arguments not predicates, but predicates of predicates, and so on. Again, by means of .19 analysis of problem-sentences used by the medievals such as '*Man* is a species' becomes possible (*LAS* 248–50). One has also a way of parsing sentences involving abstract names which does not commit one to Platonic realism in the matter of universals (cf. I §3). Finally it may be mentioned that all functors defined in terms of the primitive, lower-order '∈' can now be reduplicated analogously in terms of the new, higher-order 'is', and so on for the indefinitely large number of still higher cases. For example, now follows the definition of a higher-order singular identity, analogous to §4.3.10, but having verbs as arguments instead of names:

.20 $[\varphi\psi] : \varphi = \psi . \equiv . \varphi \in \psi . \psi \in \varphi$

Boethius shows himself aware of the differing semantical possibilities of 'is' ('*est*'), in effect, when he distinguishes between the sense of 'Cicero is healthy' and that of '*Man* is animal' (where '*man*' is used to 'refer' to the species) (*B* 201A–202A); the two correspond exactly to the lower and higher order '∈' respectively (cf. III §1).

A language rich in new and accurately definable parts of speech, and one which is capable of precisely delineating differences which are slurred over in pre-theoretical discourse, is now being made available. Thus, as a further example, we have:

.21 $[a\varphi] : Cl[\varphi](a) . \equiv . Cl[\![trm\langle\varphi\rangle]\!](a)$

Here '$Cl[\varphi]$', which may be read '. . . form the class determined by φ', is a proposition-forming functor for one nominal argument. The mention of 'classes' in this reading and in that suggested in connection with .18 should not be taken to imply that we thereby accept the existence of entities called 'classes' (cf. .24 below). Definition .21 will intervene at III §6. From .14, .18, and .19 we have the next thesis:

.22 $[a] . Cl[\![a]\!] \in Cl[\![a]\!]$

In contrast

.23 $[a] . a \in a$

is not a thesis but a false factual statement. (Restricted quantification persuades logicians not only to admit what is in effect the sense of .23, i.e. 'Everything exists' (e.g. *QF* 1), but also to take the latter to be a thesis.) From .22 one can plainly infer:

.24 $[a] : [\exists\varphi] . \varphi \in Cl[\![a]\!]$

This gives one acceptable sense to the principle that there are classes of whatever sorts of objects one may specify. (Here 'are' has its higher-order sense.) One inacceptable sense of the principle occurs when the variable appearing after the '∈' in .39 below is taken to be a variable for classes (cf. *QF* 90).

In conclusion an important group of deductions are presented which are relevant to the discussions which tend to centre around one version of Russell's paradox, and which at the same time happen to involve theses which will be instructive when the work of St Anselm and Burleigh on Non-being and Negation comes to be studied (III

§4). We thus have an illustration of the broad scope of Ontology. First one may deduce the theses:

.25 $[ab]: a \in b . \supset . [\exists c] . c \in a$ (.1)
.26 $[ab]: a \in b . \supset . [\exists \varphi] . \varphi(a)$ (.16)

The import of this last thesis is that a verb corresponding to a given name is always available. Now let us consider the conditions under which the reverse process (i.e. the derivation of a name from a verb) is possible:

.27 $[a\varphi]: . a \in a . \supset : a \in \text{trm}\langle\varphi\rangle . \equiv . \varphi(a)$ (.15)

The condition required, here stated in the antecedent, is that a should be an existing individual. Another consequence of .15 is:

.271 $[a\varphi]: a \in a . \varphi(a) . \supset . [\exists b] . a \in b$

Hence:

.28 $[a]: . a \in a . \supset : [\exists b] . a \in b . \equiv . [\exists \varphi] . \varphi(a)$
                                                      (.26, .271; cf. III §1.15)

(The case of 'b' on which the consequents of .271 and .28 are based is 'trm$\langle\varphi\rangle$'). However, as already noted, '$a \in a$' is not a thesis, but may in fact be false; hence the antecedent of .28 cannot be affirmed so as to give its consequent as a thesis by *modus ponendo ponens*. Indeed, in certain cases that consequent is itself false, as will now be demonstrated:

.29 $[a] . \sim (a \in \wedge)$ (§4.3.14; cf. III §4.7)
.30 $[a] . \sim (\wedge \in a)$ (.25, .29)
.31 $\wedge \subset \wedge$ (§4.3.5 and $[p] . p \supset p$; cf. III §4.17)
.32 $\subset [\![\wedge]\!] (\wedge)$ (.17, .31)
.33 $[\exists \varphi] . \varphi(\wedge)$ (.32)

(The 'φ' in question in this last thesis is, of course, the '$\subset [\![\wedge]\!]$' of .32.)

.34 $[\exists a] : [\exists \varphi] . \varphi(a) : [b] . \sim (a \in b)$

        i.e. $\wedge$ i.e. $\subset [\![\ \ ]\!]$ (.30)
        (.30)   (.32, .33)

This final thesis has been tabulated in such a way as to bring out exactly the source of its elements. Thus is concluded the demonstration that in at least one case (i.e. when a is $\wedge$), the consequent of .28

does not hold. Other ways of bringing out the consequences of .29 when combined with §4.3.1 are:

.35 $[a] : \sim (\text{ex}(a)) \, . \equiv . \, [b] \, . \sim (b \in a)$ (§4.3.1)

.36 $[\exists b] : [a] \, . \sim (a \in b)$ (.29)

.37 $[\exists a] \, . \sim (\text{ex}(a))$ (.35, .36)

.38 $[\exists a\varphi] \, . \, \varphi(a) \, . \sim (\text{ex}(a))$ (.37)

Now were one to affirm or omit, on grounds connected with the use of restricted quantification, the antecedent '$a \in a$' which figures in .27, one would then have as a thesis:

.39 $[\exists b] : [a\varphi] : a \in b \, . \equiv . \, \varphi(a)$ (cf. R3 of QF 89)

wherein the 'b' in question is the counterpart of '$\text{trm}\langle\varphi\rangle$'. But now suppose that the value '$\sim (\ldots \in a)$' is selected for 'φ', so that from .39 one has:

.40 $[\exists b] : [a] : a \in b \, . \equiv . \sim (a \in a)$

Then in view of the universal quantifier '$[a]$' one sees that .40 allows that 'b' should take the place of 'a' throughout, thus:

.41 $[\exists b] \, . \, b \in b \, . \equiv . \sim (b \in b)$

This is a contradiction which may be viewed as a version of Russell's paradox (see QF 90). It is, of course, avoided by .27, which stems from .15, the latter being in turn based on the definitional frame §4.2.2, the intuitive feasibility of which has been defended in §4.2. In other words, intuitive clarity can be maintained throughout, this version of the paradox is avoided, and *ad hoc* evasive strategems of a formalist nature shown to be needless (compare QF 90–92). This, however, is by no means even the beginning of a rigorous treatment of Russell's paradox; for an indication of such treatment, see *SA*.

Armed, therefore, with a satisfactory system of modern logic, we may now turn to the analysis of sample problems which are presented in connection with the interpretation of medieval logic and metaphysics.

Part III

APPLICATIONS

§1 SUPPOSITIO AND MODERN LOGIC

The doctrine of *suppositio* is one of the central points of interest in contemporary studies of the history of medieval logic. This interest arises from the current fascination with problems of meaning and reference. To give an exhaustive discussion of the doctrine is quite impossible at this juncture, and the present remarks are therefore limited to three main tasks. First, samples of the manners in which the medievals would convince themselves of the necessity of *some* doctrine of *suppositio* will be outlined. A brief look at the general complexion of Ockham's system of *suppositio* will then be essayed, followed by a closer inspection of some of the difficulties which are alleged to arise when an attempt is made to express certain features of that and other systems in terms of modern logic.

It is nowadays commonplace to recognise that requests for the elucidation of the meaning of names or name-like expressions in a language are, to say the least, ambiguous. The doctrine of *suppositio* is the form taken by the medieval recognition of this ambiguity. The history of the development of the doctrine has lately received its first documentation at the hands of De Rijk (*DLM*). It now suffices to note that ever since Boethius the necessity for distinguishing between the meaning (*significatio*) of a name on the one hand, and the various ways in which a name may be related to (supposit for) things on the other. Thus the meaning (*significatio*) of a name would be stated in a definitional sentence such as '*Man* is *rational animal*'. The assembling of the parts of this definition would involve truths such as '*Man* is a species', '*Animal* is a genus', and so forth. However, it soon becomes clear that the '*Man*' of '*Man* is a species' (which is the same as the '*Man*' of '*Man* is *rational animal*') is not the same as the 'man' of, say, 'Socrates is a man'. Thus Boethius reminds us that while one can say that an individual animal is either wise or stupid, or that an individual man is either sick or well, these contrary alternatives do

47

not apply to *animal* in so far as it is a genus, nor to *man* in so far as it is a species (*B* 201–2).

In order to account for this discrepancy, one may say that 'man' is related to (supposits for) things in at least two different ways, notwithstanding the presupposed constancy of the meaning (*significatio*) of this name throughout all its occurrences. For example, as has been implied in I §3, one might recognise the '*Man*' of '*Man* is a species' and '*Man* is *rational animal*' as being more verb-like than name-like in such contexts; although this suggestion has appeared in our own day (*LAS* 248–9) it also occurs in Aquinas and others (cf. §6 below). On this basis, using '**h**' for 'man' ('*homo*'), '**a**' for 'animal', '**r**' for 'rational', and '... ∩ ...' as the nominal conjunction '... and ...' defined at .7 below, one may then analyse the last-mentioned of these problem-sentences as

.1 $\text{Cl}[\![\mathbf{h}]\!] \in \text{Cl}[\![\mathbf{a} \cap \mathbf{r}]\!]$ (cf. II §5.19, §5.16)

Thus would the semi-formal suggestion of the Introduction (I §3) to the effect that definitional sentences involved a verb-flanked 'is' (cf. I §3.4, II §5.19) rather than a name-flanked one (cf. I §3.3, II §2.211) be given more systematic effect.

In fact .1 is one way of accounting for what was known as 'simple supposition' (*suppositio simplex*) in the medieval *suppositio* doctrine. It enables one to distinguish between 'man' at the formal, definitional, level (as in .1) and 'man' as the completion of an 'is' flanked by names (as in 'Socrates is a man'). However, .1 would only suffice for certain interpretations of simple *suppositio*. Ockham, for instance, would insist that in this context we have not only a recondite *way* in which a name can be related to (supposit for) objects, but also a pre-theoretically unsuspected *thing* which the name 'man' stands for. This thing is a mental object, an 'intention of the mind', or what would nowadays be called a 'concept' (cf. *OSL* I 178). Without going further into this matter, however, one may at least realise along with the medievals that something more than an account of meaning (*significatio*) is needed if the ways in which names and name-like expressions function in various contexts are to be accounted for.

Since certain difficulties in the logical analysis of Ockham's account of *suppositio* have arisen recently, it will be convenient to reproduce his account of the matter as it occurs in chs 63 to 67 of pt I of *OSL*. In this way an impression of the general complexion of a medieval *suppositio* doctrine may be gained, and the way opened for a demonstration of the uses of the Ontology described in Part II above. Thus, for Ockham *suppositio* may in the first place be **proper** or **improper**. The latter occurs when a name is used metaphorically or in a figure of speech, e.g. when the name 'lion' is applied to a human being

because of his bravery, as in 'Roland is a lion'. **Proper** *suppositio* has
its first main division based on the principle that on the one hand
a name may stand for that which it signifies, while on the other it
may not. In the former case one has **personal** *suppositio*, the divisions
of which will be dealt with shortly; in the second case one may have
either **simple** *suppositio* (as has 'man' in '*Man* is a species') or **material**
suppositio (as has '"man"' when we say '"Man" is a word composed
of three letters'). Of these two the first has already been briefly
discussed above, and the second is similar to the contemporary
distinction between the mention of a word and the use of that word.

In the divisions of **personal** *suppositio* one first has the distinction
between **discrete** and **common** *suppositio*. The former occurs in a case
such as that of 'Socrates' in the sentence 'Socrates is a man'; here
we have a direct reference to the individual Socrates, hence the term
'discrete' used in the characterisation of this sort of case (*OSL* I 189).
It is in connection with common *suppositio* that controversy has arisen
as to the possibility of expressing Ockham's doctrine in terms of some
modern system of logic. According to this author, **common** *suppositio*
is of two sorts, namely **determinate** and **confused**. In both these cases,
the sense of the general term (shared name) whose type of *suppositio*
is being decided is illuminated by means of what is known as a
descensus, i.e. making explicit, by reference to individual objects to
which the term in question applies, of a consequence of the proposition
in which that term occurs. For example, given that some man is
rational, the status of 'man' in this proposition may be clarified by
noting that one may thence infer that either this man is rational or
that man is rational, and so on throughout all the men (*OSL* I
190.20.22; note how this association of somehood and disjunction
parallels that found in modern quantification theory, as in II §2.25
above). Here we have a *descensus* to individuals which is *disjunctive*
(in that its units are related by 'or') and *propositional* (in that its
disjuncts are each propositional units such as 'this man is rational').
In contrast, one may in some cases have a *descensus* which while still
propositional in the sense just described, nevertheless involves a *conjunction* of the propositional units. For example, given 'Every man
is animal', the status of 'man' in this proposition may be clarified
by making explicit the proposition's consequence that this man is
animal and that man is animal, and so on throughout all the men
(*OSL* I 191.66.71; once again, note how this association of allhood
and conjunction parallels that found in modern quantification theory,
as in II §2.25 above).

Finally, one may have a *descensus* which although *disjunctive* in
nature (in that, as in the first case described, its units are related by
'or') nevertheless has disjuncts which are *nominal* units. Thus, in

respect of 'animal' in the proposition 'Every man is animal' one has the *descensus* 'hence every man is this animal or that animal or . . .' (and so on throughout all the animals) (*OSL* I 191.58.59). In this case the *descensus* is to a *single* proposition having as its predicate term a name compounded out of disjunctively connected nominal expressions such as 'this animal', 'that animal', and so on.

Thus far, then, in the discussion of common *suppositio* we have come across three types of *descensus* which may be briefly described in the ways suggested above, namely:

(i) disjunctive propositional;
(ii) conjunctive propositional;
(iii) disjunctive nominal.

The fourth possibility which is theoretically possible, i.e. the conjunctive nominal *descensus*, does not enter into the sort of case with which we are at present concerned.

Let us now list some of the theses which correspond to the inferences authorised by the various types of *descensus* described by Ockham: the term whose *suppositio* is undergoing scrutiny is in each case italicised:

.2   If some *man* is animal then this *man* is animal or that *man* is
         animal or . . . (Disjunctive propositional *descensus* relating
         to the subject term of a particular affirmative proposition);
         OSL I 190.35.36.

.3   If all men are *animal* then each man is either this *animal* or
         that *animal* or . . . (Disjunctive nominal *descensus* relating
         to predicate term of universal affirmative proposition);
         OSL I 191.58.59.

.4   If some man is *animal* then some man is this *animal* or some
         man is that *animal* or . . . (Disjunctive propositional
         descensus relating to the predicate term of a particular
         affirmative proposition); *OSL* I 190.38.39.

.5   If all *men* are animal then this *man* is animal and that *man*
         is animal and . . . (Conjunctive propositional *descensus*
         relating to the subject term of a universal affirmative
         proposition); *OSL* I 191.66.71.

Now Ockham's subdivisions of the various types of common *suppositio*, with which we are concerned, turns partly upon the triple typology of the *descensus* noted above, and partly upon a factor to which attention has not hitherto been called. This factor is the possibility of reciprocally inferring the proposition from which the *descensus* has been made by using as a premiss *one* of the (propositional) units of the *descensus*. Thus in cases .2 and .4 above one may correctly perform the reciprocal inferences having as corresponding theses the following:

> If this *man* is animal then some *man* is animal.
> If some man is this *animal* then some man is *animal*.

Under such circumstances Ockham would say that only one instance of the disjunction in question was needed to 'verify' the original proposition, and the singularity of this instance leads him to separate off those cases in which a disjunctive propositional *descensus* (cf. (i) above) is appropriate as forming a sub-class of **common** *suppositio*, namely that in which **determinate** *suppositio* applies (e.g. .2 and .4 above). On the other side of this division he places both the cases of disjunctive nominal (cf. (iii) above) and conjunctive propositional (cf. (ii) above) *descensus*. The general heading covering these last two is **confused** *suppositio*. When the first of these (the disjunctive nominal) applies as in .3 above, then we have **pure confused** or **merely confused** *suppositio* (*suppositio confusa tantum*); when the second (the conjunctive propositional) applies as in .5 then we have **distributive confused** *suppositio*.

The question has been raised (*MOS*) as to whether, as *BML* claims, the following is a proper modern logical rendering of the form of .2 as understood by Ockham:

.6 $(\exists x)\,(Fx \,.\, Gx) \supset (Fx_1 \,.\, Gx_1 \,.\, \vee \,.\, Fx_2 \,.\, Gx_2 \,.\, \vee \,. \ldots .)$

(It is understood that 'F' abbreviates the predicate '... is a man', and 'G' abbreviates the predicate '... is an animal'; the quantification is of the restricted sort (cf. II §2.25)). That it cannot be is then shown by pointing out that the consequent of .6 would also have to be the *prima facie* modern rendering of the consequent of .4, thereby missing Ockham's point that there is a difference here. More complex renderings in terms of predicate calculus enriched by identity are suggested, but rejected on account of their involving double quantification over nominal variables and a 'wastage of disjuncts' (or conjuncts) in that a consequent such as that of .6 must range over all the x's and not just all the men, as does the consequent of .2. The second issue raised in *MOS* is as to whether Boehner's reasons for alleging that modern logic and Ockham's part company because the former has nothing parallel to .3 are adequate; the conclusion reached, after an attempt to render the consequent of .5 in terms similar to those earlier applied in respect of that of .4, is that in all the cases in question, i.e. .2 to .5 above, the basic trouble is that 'Ockham quantifies over terms, whereas modern logicians quantify over variables'; *ergo* modern logic is here inadequate.

The complaint that modern logic cannot analyse certain theses or

5

forms of expression which occur in medieval logic has become a
constantly recurring commonplace in the recent histories of logic; the
offending items are dismissed as idiosyncratic (e.g. *homo est species*
'*Man* is a species'), or even as nonsense (as in the case of 'All men
exist'). The discussion just summarised attempts to diagnose exactly
what the reason for this kind of failure amounts to in the cases
described. I want to suggest that such complaints and diagnoses are
based on an excessively narrow view of what 'modern logic' is. After
all, if it fails to accommodate itself to innocent little truths like 'All
men exist', small wonder that the slightly more complex truths of
medieval logic should elude it. I shall now show the perfectly straight-
forward analyses of the problem-theses in question which are fur-
nished by Ontology, and which do full justice to Ockham's position.
This system of course by no means abrogates the perfectly reputable
predicate calculus in terms of which the discussion was originally
based.

Given the functors of strong inclusion ('... $\sqsubset$ ...') defined at II
§4.4, and partial inclusion ('... $\triangle$ ...') defined at II §4.6, we now
also need a nominal form of conjunction ('and') definable thus:

.7 $[abc] : c \in a \cap b . \equiv . c \in a . c \in b$

Further, the following thesis serves to characterise nominal disjunction ('or'); it follows from the definition of the latter:

.8 $[abc] : . c \in a \cup b . \equiv : c \in a . \vee . c \in b$

Finally, C. Lejewski's suggestion that compounds such as 'this man',
'that animal', etc. are nominal expressions formed by means of the
functor defined in .7, and each have the shared name in question and
the ambiguous proper name 'this' (or 'that') as component arguments,
may be adopted (*LAS* 250–3). The symbols 'x_1', 'x_2', and so forth
are now used as typographical abbreviations of these ambiguous
proper names, the indices serving merely to reflect this ambiguity. The
following are then the counterparts of .2, .3, .4, and .5 respectively:

.9 $[ab] : . a \triangle b . \supset . x_1 \cap a \in b . \vee . x_2 \cap a \in b . \vee .$
          $x_3 \cap a \in b . \vee . \ldots$
.10 $[ab] : a \sqsubset b . \supset . a \sqsubset x_1 \cap b \cup x_2 \cap b \cup x_3 \cap b \cup \ldots$
.11 $[ab] : . a \triangle b . \supset . a \triangle x_1 \cap b . \vee . a \triangle x_2 \cap b . \vee .$
          $a \triangle x_3 \cap b . \vee . \ldots$
.12 $[ab] : a \sqsubset b . \supset . x_1 \cap a \in b . x_2 \cap a \in b . x_3 \cap a \in b . \ldots$

It is in this fashion that modern logic can surmount not only all
the problems of analysis described above, but also the allegedly crucial
difficulty that 'Ockham quantifies over terms whereas modern
logicians quantify over variables' (*MOS*). I assume that 'variables'

here refers to variables which have as their sole substituends unshared
names, and that the latitude (shared, unshared, or empty) of the names
which are allowable as substituends in my analyses (cf. II §2.252)
remedies the defect thus diagnosed, notwithstanding my uneasiness
at this expression of the diagnosis.

At the same time it is not claimed that the analyses given above
effectively dispose of *all* the problems which hover around *suppositio*
of the confused sort, and which have recently been raised, for instance
in *GRG*. Such analyses would however, appear to be proof against
an objection raised in *TLO* to the effect that they are only valid in
an Ockhamist context, wherein is accepted what is called 'the two-
name theory of predication'. This objection would appear to be based
on one of the various possible ways in which the sense of the primitive
'. . . ∈ . . .' of Ontology can be explained, i.e. by representing it as
a functor which forms a proposition from two names (cf. II §2.211).
A sentence such as 'Socrates is white' is thus seen as composed of
the verb '. . . is . . .' completed by two names. It is then assumed that
this latter description excludes an alternative one, according to which
the same sentence would be represented as composed of a name
('Socrates') and a verb ('is white'). This alternative description, with
its structure of the form '$\varphi(x)$', is alleged to be necessary in order
to show the 'disparity of semantic category which holds between the
subject and the predicate', and to be the one drawn from Frege which
best agrees with Thomist analyses of predication as opposed to
Ockhamist ones which favour a 'two-name' theory.

This objection seems to imply that the '$\varphi(x)$' form is not available
in Ontology for the purpose of analysing simple sentences such as
the ones now in question. This of course is not the case. Further,
given the material of Part II above, it is easy to exemplify some of
the manners in which Ontology can deal with the relations between
names and verbs by recalling definitions II §5.16 and II §5.15, thus:

.13 $[ab] : \in[\![b]\!] (a) . \equiv . a \in b$
.14 $[a\varphi] : a \in \text{trm}\langle\varphi\rangle . \equiv . a \in a . \varphi(a)$

From these one may infer:

.15 $[a] : . a \in a . \supset : [\exists\varphi] . \varphi(a) . \equiv . [\exists b] . a \in b$ (cf. II §5.28)

The functor defined by .13 is '$\in[\![\ ]\!] (\ )$', a functor-forming functor
for one argument which is a name, the functor thus formed, when
completed by one nominal argument, yielding a proposition. It is thus
one of many instances of the 'φ' of the preferred and allegedly Thomist
form which Ontology makes available; by means of this definition
one has the guarantee of a verb corresponding to every name, and

hence of a '$\varphi(x)$' form corresponding to every 'two-name' form of the type '$a \in b$'. Conversely, .14 guarantees a name ('trm$\langle \quad \rangle$', read as 'term satisfying . . .' or '. . . -er') for every verb (i.e. value of 'φ'). Ordinary language has plenty of instances of such verb-name correlations (e.g. '. . . rules' with 'ruler', '. . . runs' with 'runner', and so on); all that is being done here is to generalise something that is quite familiar. Hence, as .15 illustrates, systems of the Frege–Russell type are in fact contained within Ontology. There is thus no reason at all why Ontology should not serve for the analysis of the theses of those medieval authors who reject the 'two-name theory of predication'. By such analyses their assertions are made intelligible in the light of a single primitive term (e.g. '. . . $\in$ . . .', or any such other as may be chosen), and I fail to see how analytic intelligibility can be carried any further. Examples of such analyses in non-Ockhamist contexts may be seen in §5 and §6 below.

However, owing to the usual formalist manner in which it is customary to present logic nowadays, it is not surprising that Leśniewskian systems should be taken to be of this formalist type, and a further objection to analyses in terms of such systems raised as follows: 'A logic differs from an uninterpreted calculus in that, at least according to many logical theorists (including the medieval logicians under discussion) a logic is always developed with a view to an interpretation. It must be developed with a view to expressing what can truly be said about the world' (*TLO* 363). In fact the view of logic propounded is exactly the one adopted by Leśniewski (cf. II §0.00, *LR*, *LLL*). Hence the definitions given above are *not* 'simply a matter of translation, a matter of finding a notation by means of which we can write up certain forms of sentences in a spoken or written language', but are 'truths about the world'. In view of all this, I fail to see how 'the representation of predication in a Thomist or Fregean system' (e.g. in terms of the functor on the left-hand side of .13 above) 'properly reflects the relation of inherence of a form in the matter of which it is the form in that about which the proposition speaks in a way in which its representation in Ockham's' (i.e. the right-hand side of .13) 'or Leśniewski's system' (i.e. *either* side of .13) 'would not' (*TLO* 363).

It seems to me highly probable that the clue to the only difficulty which can now obstruct the 'Thomist' logician's accepting analyses in terms of Leśniewski's Ontology lies in the ways of speaking favoured in this last quotation ('inherence of a form . . .' and the like). These ways of speaking are connected with the statement of the truth-conditions of sentences such as 'Socrates is a man'; '$\varphi(x)$', it will be alleged, reflects better the way in which the Thomist would prefer to express those truth-conditions than does '$a \in b$'. However, until

it is shown, with reference to some theory of truth-condition statements, that the two manners of stating truth-conditions are not
inferentially equivalent, then the argument tends to be somewhat
indecisive. In the absence of such a theory, one can only speak in
a speculative and fragmentary fashion, but I am, as it happens, inclined
to believe that *in its original historical setting* the 'two-name' statement
of the truth-conditions was in fact designed to exclude certain quite
valid standpoints which the Thomists, with their rival statements, were
concerned to defend. To that extent, and in that setting, the latter
were justified in eschewing the 'two-name' theory, as I shall attempt
to confirm briefly below. But to make the possible (not necessary)
acceptance of the 'two-name' statement of truth-conditions into a
touchstone which has the magical property of signifying for all time
and relative to all systems, the exclusion of those valid standpoints,
is surely a move of which we should be exceedingly wary.

In my opinion that technical terminology of 'form' and its like
which is alleged to be excluded by the 'two-name' theory in fact
represents a justified artificialisation of natural language for the purpose of expressing truths about how things are—truths involving
semantical categories too recondite to be expressed in unalloyed
natural language. That this is so may be gathered in part from I §3
above, and from §5 and §6 below. Hence, if the Ockhamist's preferred
statement of truth-conditions was designed to exclude such expressions, and §5 below already suggests that this would be a reasonable
surmise, then that form of statement is, in its original context, certainly
to be deprecated. But if, as is perfectly obvious to anyone acquainted
with the system, Leśniewski's Ontology does *not* exclude truths involving such recondite semantical categories, then it is pointless to
urge against it the quite accidental coincidence that it is possible (but
not at all necessary) to outline the truth or sense conditions of its
primitive term in the same form of words as was used by the medieval
two-name theorists. As has been shown, this form of words could,
if preferred, be dropped and replaced by one which revolves around
the '$\varphi(x)$' form.

However, finally and most importantly, this controversy has nothing at all to do with Ontology as such. The statement of the truth-
conditions of the primitive term is *not* a part of Ontology, and
Leśniewski insisted that *any* method of putting over the sense of the
primitive term could be adopted: gesticulational, choreographic,
verbal, or whatever happened, in the circumstances, to promise to be
most effective. For most people, specification in terms of traditional
grammatical categories seems to be effective enough, but this is by
no means sacrosanct: anything may be pressed into service (cf. II
§2.1).

§2   ANSELMIAN REGRESSES*

A tactic sometimes employed in philosophical argument involves showing that the position of one's opponent commits him to an infinite regress. On the assumption that the regress in question is unacceptable, such a consequence refutes the opponent's argument. A process of this sort can most obviously be used to suggest superfluity in the terms of a definition, as in the following example from St Anselm's dialogue on paronymy (*De Grammatico*):

.1   TUTOR. . . . if *literate* is *man displaying literacy*, then wherever *literate* appears the words *man displaying literacy* may be correctly substituted for it.

MAGISTER. . . . *si* grammaticus *est* homo sciens grammaticam *ubicumque ponitur* grammaticus, *apte ponitur* homo sciens grammaticam.

STUDENT. That's right.

DISCIPULUS. *Ita est.*

T. Hence if it is appropriate to say, 'Socrates is a literate man', it is equally appropriate to say, 'Socrates is a man displaying literacy man'.

M. *Si igitur apte dicitur: Socrates est homo grammaticus, apte quoque dicitur: Socrates est homo homo sciens grammaticam.*

S. So it follows.

D. *Consequitur.*

T. But every man displaying literacy is a literate man.

M. *Omnis autem homo sciens grammaticam est homo grammaticus.*

S. Yes.

D. *Ita est.*

T. Thus Socrates, who is a man displaying literacy man, is a literate man man, and since a literate is a man displaying literacy, it follows that Socrates is a man displaying literacy man man, and so on to infinity. . . . It

M. *Socrates igitur qui est homo homo sciens grammaticam, est homo homo grammaticus. Et quoniam grammaticus est homo sciens grammaticam, consequitur ut Socrates sit homo homo homo sciens grammaticam,*

* It would be unfortunate if the comparatively dense nature of this section's subject-matter and mode of presentation were to make it into a *pons asinorum*, obstructing advance into the later sections. Readers who experience undue difficulty herein may pass immediately to the later sections, each of which can be read as a unity largely independent of the others.

has now been sufficiently proved that *literate* does not signify man.	*et sic in infinitum. . . . Iam satis probatum est quia non significat hominem.*
s. Quite sufficiently.	D. *Satis.*
T. What then is left?	M. *Quid ergo restat?*
s. It can only signify . . . *displaying literacy.*	D. *Ut non significet aliud quam* scientem grammaticam.

(*HDG* 4.2414, 4.31)

The Tutor is here arguing, following a pattern suggested by Aristotle, that an account of the meaning of *grammaticus* 'literate' should not comprise a mention of its constant referent, i.e. man. He uses the regress which results from such a mention in order to refute the Student's contention.

The aim of the present section is to sketch the general nature of the field of Anselm's dialogue and then to inspect in some detail the logical significance of yet another argument from regress which occurs in the same work.

Grammaticus 'literate' is for Anselm an example of what are known as denominative names or paronyms. It is a familiar fact of current English that most adjectives have a corresponding abstract noun, as 'white' has 'whiteness', 'smooth' has 'smoothness', 'literate' has 'literacy', and so on. The concrete members of such pairs serve as examples of the paronyms with which we are now concerned. They receive their title of 'paronym' or its alternative 'denominative name' because of their supposed derivation from their corresponding and partly equiform abstract nouns (cf. *HL* §3.123, *HDG* ch. IV, *HW* and *HAN*). The problem of the signification of paronyms lies essentially in the question as to whether an account of their *meaning* should at the same time involve an account of their *reference*. If one concentrates on the adjectives which constitute the main body of the paronyms, then, as H. W. B. Joseph says, 'their invention implies the consideration of some quality or character in the thing in abstraction from the rest of the thing's nature' (*JL* 38). Under such circumstances one is tempted to say that the corresponding abstract noun is a sufficient account of their meaning, and any mention of the things to which they happen to refer is superfluous (*HL* §3.131). Such appears to have been the position of the logical tradition of which Anselm was the inheritor (*HL* §3.124). On the other hand, if one considers certain paronyms which constantly happen to qualify only a single species of being, as in the case of Anselm's 'literate', which is used only of human beings, then the result might be the demand that some mention of this constant referent should be included in any account of what this and other paronyms signify. This sort of demand would be backed up in Anselm's own day by the thesis inherited from the grammarians, in particular Priscian, to the effect that *all* names (of which adjectives were considered a species) signify both a substance (e.g. *man*, in the case of 'literate') and a quality (e.g. literacy); *HDG* §4.109, *HL* §3.124. J. S. Mill, with his doctrine that all 'terms' have both connotation and denotation, appears to be somewhat on the side of Priscian (*HDG* §4.314).

In pursuance of the logical, rather than the grammatical tradition, Anselm holds that there *is* a difference between the ways in which adjectival words and substance-words signify (*HDG* §5.2, *HL* §3, *HAN*). Any account of the meaning of paronyms (which are now assumed to exclude substance-words such as 'man') ought to depict them as being completely open as regards the type of object to which they may apply. Thus, although as a matter of fact 'literate' has always been *used* in respect of human beings, this should not affect the account given of its *meaning*, if 'meaning' is taken in a strict technical sense (*HL* §2.13.1, *HDG* 4.232–2.2341). This is the background to the regress-argument quoted at .1 above, and Anselm's conclusion at this juncture could be expressed:

.2   *grammaticus est habens grammaticam*   (*HDG* 4.31, 4.700)
        a literate is a haver of literacy
        or
        literate is . . . having literacy

Anselm strains all his powers of explanation to suggest that something like the second English version of .2, with its gapped (i.e. functorial) formulation, is a true representation of the thesis he intends to express. Thus he expels by means of various arguments (of which .1 is one) the *homo* 'man' part from the Student's suggested definition of *grammaticus* 'literate' as *homo habens* (or *sciens*) *grammaticam* 'man having (*or* displaying) literacy' (*HDG* 4.31). Again, as we are to see below, while accepting, in a parallel case, that *albus est aliquid habens albedinem* '(a) white is something having whiteness' is a truth, he will nevertheless insist that *albus est habens albedinem* 'white is . . . having whiteness' is the proper expression of what he intends to say. The expulsion of even the colourless *aliquid* 'something' from the meaning of 'white' shows that any clue as to the nature of the referent of the word which may be given by the gender (in this case masculine) of the Latin version of the word must be considered irrelevant; cf. *HDG* §2.32. This expulsion corresponds, of course, to the removal of 'man' which is arrived at in .1.

The issue can be further contextualised and stated thus: it was pointed out in I §3 that decisions on the appropriateness of definitions framed according to the canons of Aristotle and Boethius can involve resource to statements such as *grammaticus est species* '*literate* is a species' (*HDG* 4.2411), *grammaticus est qualitas* '*literate* is a quality' (*HDG* 4.603), and *homo est genus* '*man* is a genus' (*HDG* 4.2411), in which the *est* 'is' is plainly peculiar and problematical in so far as it is not the same *est* 'is' as we have in *Socrates est philosophus* 'Socrates is a philosopher'. In terms of Leśniewski's Ontology at least some of these problem-sentences may be elucidated in terms of the verb-flanked '. . . is . . .' defined at II §5.19 (cf. *LAS* 248–9 and I §3.4 above). Such an interpretation, with its incomplete, functorial arguments for the '. . . is . . .' (and for functors defined in terms of that '. . . is . . .') is at any rate one which allows for that openness of meaning for paronyms which Anselm so urgently requires, as indicated by .1 and the contentions summarised at the close of the last paragraph. It is perhaps with some intuition of the special logical grammar which his thesis requires that Anselm, here dealing with a question of definition, holds that .2 can yield assertions such as *grammaticus est grammatica* '*literate* is literacy' which, though required in this definitional context, do not cohere with *usus loquendi* 'ordinary language'. In this respect (i.e. in having consequences not cohering with ordinary usage) .2 would be related to the problematical sentences quoted above and which involve open verb-like arguments for their '. . . is . . .'; these are the sort of arguments which Anselm appears to require for the *est* 'is' of .2. The Student, on the other hand, insists on interpreting assertions such as .2, notwithstanding their occurrence in the context of definitional discussion, as being of a more familiar sort, i.e. as involving an *est* 'is' having two *nominal* arguments (as does 'Socrates is a philosopher'); cf. *HL* §3.221. The Student's claim that the referent 'man' should be included in the definition of 'literate' appears to be an index of his insistence on the non-verb-like, merely nominal, interpretation of the completions of the *est* 'is' of .2, an interpretation which is coverable by the first of the two English translations which accompany .2.

What we may here be faced with, therefore, are two possibilities for the interpretation of names or name-like expressions: they may indeed be names (like the 'man' of 'Jack is a man') but sometimes are better construed as verb-like functors (like the 'man' of '*man* is a species'). This contrast comes out well when the statement:

.3   *albus est (idem quod) habens albedinem*
        (a) white is (the same as) a haver of whiteness
        or
        white is (the same as) . . . having whiteness

is discussed (*HDG* 4.8). For the Tutor this is in the present context of the same type as .2, in that it resembles the latter throughout except in so far as the paronym *albus* 'white' has replaced *grammaticus* 'literate'; as an alternative exemplification of his thesis he therefore accepts it. However, the Student insists on interpreting .3 as involving an 'is' whose two arguments are nominal (cf. the first English translation annexed to .3) and the Tutor shows that this supposition leads to an infinite regress. Now should it turn out that an analysis of this regress confirms in detail Anselm's intuition that .2 and .3, interpreted as having non-nominal functorial arguments for their 'is' (cf. the second English translation annexed to .3), need not give rise to regress, then the conjecture that he appreciates the unusual semantical categories involved in the situation will be to some extent confirmed. Here now is the discussion which centres around .3:

4.   STUDENT. As *white* is equivalent to *having whiteness*, it does not determinately signify this or that thing having whiteness, such as a body; rather it signifies indeterminately some thing having whiteness. This is because a white is either that which has whiteness or that which has not whiteness; but that which has not whiteness is not white, so that a white is that which has whiteness. Further, since everything which has whiteness must needs be something, a white must be something which has whiteness, or something having whiteness. Finally *white* signifies either something having whiteness or nothing; but nothing cannot be conceived to have whiteness, hence *white* must signify something having whiteness (cf. §4 below).

DISCIPULUS. Albus *cum sit idem quod* habens albedinem, *non significat determinate hoc vel illud habens, velut corpus, sed indeterminate aliquid habens albedinem. Albus enim aut est qui habet albedinem, aut qui non habet. Sed qui non habet albedinem non est albus. Albus igitur est qui habet albedinem. Quare quoniam omnis qui albedinem habet non nisi aliquid est, necesse est ut albus sit aliquid quod habet albedinem, aut aliquid habens albedinem. Denique* albus *aut aliquid significat habens albedinem aut nihil. Sed nihil non potest intelligi habens albedinem. Necesse est ergo ut* albus *significet aliquid habens albedinem* (cf. §4 below).

TUTOR. The question is not whether everything which is white is something, or whether it is that which has, but whether the word *white* contains in its signification the expression *something*, or *that which has*, in the way that *man* contains *animal*, with the consequence that in the same way as *man* is *rational mortal animal*, so also *white* is *something having whiteness* or *that which has whiteness*. Now many things are necessary to the being of anything you care to mention, and yet are not signified by the name of the thing in question. For example, every animal must be coloured as well as either rational or irrational, yet the name *animal* signifies none of these things. Hence although there is no white which is not something having whiteness or that which has whiteness, nevertheless *white* need not signify these facts.

Nevertheless, let us suppose that *white* can signify *something having whiteness*. Now *something having whiteness* is the same as *something white*.

MAGISTER. *Non agitur utrum omnis qui est albus sit aliquid aut sit qui habet, sed utrum hoc nomen sua significatione contineat hoc quod dicitur aliquid aut qui habet—sicut* homo *continet* animal—*ut quomodo* homo *est* animal rationale mortale, *ita* albus *sit* aliquid habens albedinem *aut* qui habet albedinem. *Multa namque necesse est rem quamlibet esse, quae tamen rei eiusdem nomine non significantur. Nam omne animal necesse est coloratum esse et rationale aut irrationale, nomen tamen animalis nihil horum significat. Quare licet albus non sit nisi aliquid habens aut qui habet albedinem, non tamen necesse est ut* albus *hoc significet.*

Ponamus enim quod albus *sive* album *significet* aliquid habens albedinem. *Sed* aliquid habens albedinem *non est aliud quam* aliquid album.

s. It must be so.

D. *Non potest aliud esse.*

T. *White* therefore always signifies *something white*.

M. Albus *igitur sive* album *semper significat* aliquid album.

s. Quite so.

D. *Ita sit.*

T. So that wherever *white* appears it is always correct to substitute *something white* for *white*.

M. *Ubi ergo ponitur* albus *vel* album *recte semper accipitur pro* albo aliquid album.

S. That follows.

D. *Consequitur.*

T. Hence when *something white* is used, the double expression *something something white* is also correct; when the double is correct, so also is the triple, and so on to infinity.

M. *Ergo ubi dicitur* aliquid album, *recte quoque dicitur bis:* aliquid aliquid album; *et ubi bis, ibi et ter, et hoc infinite.*

S. This is a derivable absurdity.

D. *Consequens et absurdum est hoc.*

(*HDG* 4.800–4.8120)

(The translation of *qui* 'who/that' has here been rendered in such a fashion as to give that neutrality after which Anselm is evidently striving, and which has been remarked on above; cf. *HDG* §2.32.) The contrasting logical levels presupposed by the Tutor and Student in this passage may be approached with reference to the Ontology described in Part II. In the first place, to the axiom and definitions given in II §5 one may add:

.5 $\qquad [\varphi\psi] : . \, \varphi \circ \psi . \equiv : [\chi] : \chi \in \varphi . \equiv . \chi \in \psi$

This defines a higher-order weak identity, analogous to II §4.3.12, but based on the '$\in$' of II §5.19. It thus takes as its arguments the gapped functorial expressions which Anselm would seem to require (cf. .20, .21 below). It is at this level that we assume the Tutor to pitch his interpretation of .3.

Let us now consider the nominal expressions required for the expression of the Student's interpretation of .3. These will operate not at the level of the higher order '$\in$' or '$\circ$' mentioned in the last paragraph, but rather at the level of the primitive, lower-order '$\in$' which figures in the axiom of Ontology presented in Part II. If for present purposes we assume that abstract nouns are logically more akin to verbs than to nouns (an assumption to be developed in §5 and §6 below), then given the abstract noun *albedo* 'whiteness', hereunder abbreviated as 'ω', a corresponding nominal expression, i.e. *habens albedinem* 'whiteness haver' or *aliquid habens albedinems* 'something having whiteness' ('trm$\langle\omega\rangle$'), counterpart of the first English translation annexed to .3, can be introduced by means of II §5.15:

.6 $\qquad [a] : a \in \text{trm}\langle\omega\rangle . \equiv . a \in a . \omega(a)$

Next *albus* 'white', the corresponding concrete form hereunder abbreviated as '**w**', could be introduced thus:

.7 $[a] : a \in \mathbf{w} \,.\, \equiv \,.\, a \in \mathrm{trm}\langle\omega\rangle$ (cf. .6)

Definitions II §5.16 and II §5.15 may now also be used to give the sense of *aliquid album* 'something that is-white'; for the predicate 'is-white' ('$\in[\![\mathbf{w}]\!]$') may be formed from the name '**w**' thus:

.8 $[a] : \in[\![\mathbf{w}]\!]\,(a) \,.\, \equiv \,.\, a \in \mathbf{w}$ (cf. .7 and II §5.16)

and this predicate in turn used to form the nominal expression 'term satisfying is-white' ('$\mathrm{trm}\langle\in[\![\mathbf{w}]\!]\rangle$'), i.e. *aliquid album* 'something white', thus:

.9 $[a] : a \in \mathrm{trm}\langle\in[\![\mathbf{w}]\!]\rangle \,.\, \equiv \,.\, a \in a \,.\, \in[\![\mathbf{w}]\!]\,(a)$ (cf. .8 and II §5.15)

Having thus made this excursion into some theorems of the theory of 'white' we are equipped to deal with the nominal expressions undergoing discussion in .4 in so far as they involve nominal arguments. (The more complex renderings of some of these nominal arguments (§6 below) are unnecessary for present purposes.)

As regards the Tutor's interpretation of .3 (the counterpart of the second of the English translations thereto annexed) it has already been noted (§1 of this part) that the functor '$\mathrm{Cl}[\![\ ]\!]$', defined II §5.18, can be used to account for certain cases such as the ones with which we are concerned in his thesis, i.e. cases in which names or name-like expressions occur in the natural language, but have to be construed logically as being verb-like in character. Thus, to revert to an example already mentioned, the *homo* 'man' of '*homo est species*' 'man is a species' could in fact be rendered (using '**h**' for *homo* 'man') as '$\mathrm{Cl}[\![\mathbf{h}]\!]$' in order to fit it to become an argument of the higher-order *est* 'is' here involved, and which can be analysed as the higher-order '$\in$' (taking verb-like functors, not names as arguments) defined at II §5.19 above. (This suggestion stems from *LAS* 248–9; cf. also *HDG* §5.32, *HDG* §6.3126, *HL* §3.221, and *HAN*, as well as §6 below.) It is hence in terms of '$\mathrm{Cl}[\![\ ]\!]$', also a suitable argument for the functor defined at .5, that the Tutor's contentions in .4 will be analysed below (cf. .19). It will also be useful to assume the following thesis, provable from the axiom and from the definitions quoted after it:

.10 $[ab] : \mathrm{Cl}[\![a]\!] \in \mathrm{Cl}[\![b]\!] \,.\, \equiv \,.\, \mathrm{Cl}[\![a]\!] \circ \mathrm{Cl}[\![b]\!]$

(cf. II §5.18, §5.19 and .5 above.) This thesis shows us how, at this higher-order level, and with the arguments ('$\mathrm{Cl}[\![\ ]\!]$') now in question, an *est* 'is' amounts to an *est idem quod* 'is the same as'. This point is made in case anyone should have qualms about the use of the higher-order '$\circ$' to translate the higher-order 'is' (as at .19 below).

As a preliminary summary of .4 we may say that the Student opts for an interpretation of .3 such that the arguments of its *est* (*idem quod*) 'is (the same as)' are supposed to be unavoidably nominal. Forthwith the Tutor rejoins that such an interpretation, though not giving rise to falsehood, is nevertheless irrelevant in the present context, and shows that it leads to an infinite regress which his own (functorial and non-nominal) interpretation of those arguments avoids. This he construes as evidence for the rejection of the Student's interpretation (*HDG* 4.81).

In the detailed expansion of this summary which now follows the literary variants of *est* (*idem quod*) 'is (the same as)' which occur in the text of .4 (i.e. *non est aliud quam* 'is no other than' *recte semper accipitur pro* 'is always rightly taken in the place of', and so on) and their *de voce* 'utterance-related' alternatives (e.g. *significat* 'signifies') are hereunder uniformly replaced by the sign of weak identity, namely 'o' (cf. II §4.3.12). This would seem justified in view of the definitional context within which we are working. And although, in the text, it may be observed that Anselm carefully distinguishes between questions about meaning and questions about things, a full perusal of his dialogue will reveal that he would have no objection to the telescoping of these in the way which is implied by our use of 'o'.

Thus in .4 we find the Student giving to .3 the following interpretation:

.11   *Album est aliquid habens albedinem*
        A white (object) is something having whiteness

This would appear to be intended to bring out the nominal nature of the arguments of *est* 'is', and so to be of the form:

.12 $\mathbf{w} \circ \text{trm}\langle\omega\rangle$ (cf. .6, .7 and II §4.3.12, II § 5.15)

He then accepts

.13   *aliquid habens albedinem* ○ *aliquid album*
        something having whiteness ○ something white

This, in terms of the expressions made available above, may be interpreted as:

.14 $\text{trm}\langle\omega\rangle \circ \text{trm}\langle\in[\![\mathbf{w}]\!]\rangle$ (cf. .7, .9)

Then from identities .11 and .13 the Student finds himself committed to the following further identity:

.15   *albus* ○ *aliquid album*
        white ○ something white

which amounts to:

.16 $\mathbf{w} \circ \mathrm{trm}\langle\in[\![\mathbf{w}]\!]\rangle$ (cf. .7, .9)

As already remarked above, the gender of *albus* 'white' is here im-
material, so that the identity given in .16 can plainly be used to effect
substitutions of *aliquid album* 'something white' wherever *albus* (or
album) 'white' appears, even in .16 itself. One can hence infer:

.17   *aliquid album* $\circ$ *aliquid aliquid album*
         something white $\circ$ something something white

The corresponding operation in the artificial language, i.e .the sub-
stitution of '$\mathrm{trm}\langle\in[\![\mathbf{w}]\!]\rangle$' for '$\mathbf{w}$' throughout .16 and in accordance with
.16 itself, yields:

.18 $\mathrm{trm}\langle\in[\![\mathbf{w}]\!]\rangle \circ \mathrm{trm}\langle\in[\![\mathrm{trm}\langle\in[\![\mathbf{w}]\!]\rangle]\!]\rangle$

The regresses initiated in .17 and .18 can plainly, by .15 and .16
respectively, be continued to infinity. It is on these grounds that the
Tutor concludes that .11 must be rejected as an interpretation of the
definition of *albus* 'white', formulated as at .3 above. In other words,
the arguments of the *est* (*idem quod*) 'is (the same as)' of .3 must not
be taken to be nominal in nature. Following the lines suggested above,
the contrasting interpretation, involving open verb-like arguments
('Cl[   ]') of the sort which the Tutor appears to require, could read:

.19 $\mathrm{Cl}[\![\mathbf{w}]\!] \circ \mathrm{Cl}[\![\mathrm{trm}\langle\omega\rangle]\!]$

Although this interpretation is the exact higher-order correlate of .12,
the regress initiated at .16 cannot be reproduced at this level, even
though .14 and .16 are brought in as well. This regress-evasion occurs
because (as in the case of Anselm's Latin version) it is now impossible
to contrive that the first argument of .19 becomes equiform with part
of its second argument, whereas this equiformity is conceded in .16.

   As remarked above, .19 is a higher-order version of .12. By the
use of .22, which the Tutor accepts as a truth, one could infer from
.19 the higher-order analogue of .14, namely:

.20 $\mathrm{Cl}[\![\mathrm{trm}\langle\omega\rangle]\!] \circ \mathrm{Cl}[\![\mathrm{trm}\langle\in[\![\mathbf{w}]\!]\rangle]\!]$ (cf. .5)

From this, coupled with .19, one could then in turn infer:

.21 $\mathrm{Cl}[\![\mathbf{w}]\!] \circ \mathrm{Cl}[\![\mathrm{trm}\langle\in[\![\mathbf{w}]\!]\rangle]\!]$

This last is the higher-order version of the regress-generating .16. Still,
in this case an infinite regress cannot be generated by substitution
of the second argument of the '$\circ$' of .21 for any unit of that second
argument which is equiform with the first argument, since there is
now no such equiformity. In this respect .21 differs from .16.

It looks, therefore, as though Anselm's intuition that .3 (and other definitions for like paronyms) must be expressed in non-nominal terms if a regress is to be avoided has been substantiated by the analysis provided above. One may well ask, however, whether this result is of any real logical or philosophical significance. The answer is that relative to the resources of Ontology it can be seen to have very little import. For .12, .14 and .16 can be shown to be inferentially equivalent to .19, .20, and .21 respectively. Hence given .21, inference of the regress from .16 is still possible. This regress is no more vicious than the repetition of '*p*' which propositional calculus allows us to infer in '$p . \supset . p . p . p . \ldots$', for example.

From the point of view of the history of Logic, however, there *is* a lesson to be learned here. Nowadays we are in possession of systematic languages involving quantification over various types of variable for the expression of complex truths, including those required for definition. In the only slightly modified natural language of the medievals, however, recourse to a word such as *aliquid* 'something' was necessary for the expression of what we would construe as variables, and this was unreliable when exploited in contexts of any complexity (cf. §4 below). However, it is already evident that although truths such as .19 have a complicated structure which needs to be ultimately rendered in terms of the variables and quantifiers occurring in the appropriate definitions, they are nevertheless susceptible of a comparatively simple statement in what looks like natural language (e.g. .3). Hence, by insisting that formal, definitional discourse concerning the essences or 'forms' of things should involve recondite semantical categories (cf. I §3) with the sometimes consequently deviant language noted in passing in the present section, the medievals were enabled to keep their considerations on a suitably general plane without getting too much immersed in the details of quantifiers and variables with which their semi-artificial language was ill-equipped to deal. However, they lacked an efficient background system of logic in terms of which discourse at this formal level could be kept under control and explained. Thus the interrelations such as those revealed in the last paragraph between apparently conflicting theses could not be made explicit. The Student in .4, with his insistence on *aliquid* 'something', was not altogether wrong, after all. Such unnecessary mutual misunderstandings were then liable to give rise to the sort of confusion and argument at cross-purposes which we have witnessed and which are also touched upon in I §3 as well as in §5 of the present part.

The medievals, with their logical metaphysics and metaphysical logic, were working on lines which point rather in a contemporary direction, unlike some of the more disastrous efforts of intervening 'modern' philosophy. Unfortunately, they were working at about the same stage as that of a non-symbolic mathematics wherein it is necessary to remain at the level of expression exemplified in:

.22   The difference of two squared numbers is equal to the product of the sum of the two and the difference of the two.

instead of making use of variables, as in:

.23 $a^2 - b^2 = (a + b)(a - b)$

It is therefore a great pity if people now concerned (perhaps unwittingly) with projects akin to those of the medievals, still insist on remaining at the stage exemplified in .22 whereas (as the present work attempts to show) it is possible to go forward to improvements analogous to .23. Such an insistence can only result in an unnecessary continuation of the 'mock battle' picture of metaphysics, as described by Kant in the preface to the first edition of the *Critique of Pure Reason*.

§3   EXISTENCE AND INCLUSION

It is sometimes suggested that sentences of the traditional categorical form 'Every a is b' (or 'All a is b') should properly be analysed as being of the form, 'For all x, if $\varphi(x)$ then $\psi(x)$' (e.g. *RI* 162). As it stands this translation is unsatisfactory, since the predicate variables 'φ' and 'ψ' are not covered by any quantifier, and it hence has not the determinate sense possessed by the original of which it is supposed to be a translation; in fact, if one quantifies them universally, then the result is quite obviously too broad, since instances of 'φ' and 'ψ' could be just *any* predicates, as opposed to the '. . . is a' and '. . . is b' which would appear to be the ones appropriate in the case. But if one quantifies them particularly then the result is again too broad, since the exact predicates required as substituends for 'φ' and 'ψ' are not specified. In any case, with the restricted interpretation of the quantifiers, one now runs into the trouble described in Essay I of *QF*. It would therefore appear that a more satisfactory rendering of 'Every a is b' (or 'All a is b') is the one suggested by definition II §4.3.5, i.e.

.1 $[ab] :. \ a \subset b . \equiv : [c] : c \in a . \supset . c \in b$

Although this is certainly an improvement on the suggestion described above, since now any questions which may be raised concerning quantification over predicates no longer arise, and it is made clear that '. . . $\in a$' and '. . . $\in b$' are the required inner structures of 'φ' and 'ψ' respectively, it still has the disadvantage, described at length in

6

RI and elsewhere, of not allowing the traditionally valid inference from 'Every *a* is *b*' to 'Some *a* is *b*'; this is because acceptance of .1 as the version of 'Every *a* is *b*' leaves it with no existential import, whereas 'Some *a* is *b*' has such an import. It would therefore be improper to render that inference in terms of .1 (cf. *BML* 30). On this account the strong inclusion defined at II §4.3.4 seems more appropriate, i.e.

.2 $[ab]::a \sqsubset b . \equiv: . [\exists c] . c \in a : . [c] : c \in a . \supset . c \in b$

This allows the traditionally valid inference mentioned to take place, and we have hence found the means of satisfying in modern terms the requirement enunciated by Boehner: 'A scholastic universal affirmative proposition contains much more than a universal, affirmative proposition of modern logic, for it contains existential import' (*BML* 44).

However, this is by no means the end of the matter. For although .2 suffices as the foundation for the interpretation of Ockham's *descensus* criteria for the varieties of *suppositio* (cf. §1.12) it is now clear (from *WSS*, for example) that even more complex interpretations of 'Every *a* is *b*' (or 'All *a* is *b*') were envisaged by the medievals. Such complexities were apparently inspired by considerations such as the following. Consider a case of the sort of 'Every animal is living'; the word 'every' may be taken to affect the subject-term 'animal' in either of two ways. It may convey the import that every sub-species of the genus *animal* is a species of a living being, so that consequences of 'Every animal is living', thus understood, would be 'The Elephant is living', 'The Giraffe is living', 'Man is living', and so on throughout the various animal species. Under these circumstances 'every' (or 'all') would, according to William of Sherwood, be taken 'properly' and divide the 'subject' (*animal*) in respect of its *specific* parts (*WSS* 20). On the other hand, 'Every animal is living' may convey the import that every individual object of which '. . . is animal' holds is also a living being (cf. the *descensus* analysed at III §1.12). Under these circumstances 'every' or 'all' would, according to William of Sherwood, be taken 'commonly', and divide the 'subject' (*animal*) in respect of its *numerical* parts (*WSS* 20). It is evident from William of Sherwood's examples that on the second of these two interpretations a proposition of the 'Every *a* is *b*' form does have existential import, whereas on the first interpretation it does not. For instance, 'Every man is animal' can be true under that first interpretation even though no human beings exist (*WSS* 21). (The fact that *man* has, strictly speaking, no sub-species, may be neglected for the moment; this point will be referred to later.)

In the face of the situation outlined, it is clear enough that .2 above is an adequate analysis of the case wherein 'Every' is taken *commonly*.

The case wherein 'Every' is taken *properly*, with non-existential results, may be approached in two ways. First, and negatively, it may be accepted that .1, although showing *one* non-existential sense of 'Every *a* is *b*' (or 'All *a* is *b*'), nevertheless reveals for the moment no sign of the 'division into specific parts' which William requires, and hence does not appear to fill the bill. Secondly, and positively, it may help if an approach which is based directly on William's mention of species is used. We may couple this mention with the assumption that assertions concerning species such as those exemplified in the last paragraph can be analysed in terms of the higher-order, verb-flanked '∈' (II §5.19, cf. *LAS* 248–50, *HDG* §6.31 and §6.32, *HL* 102–3). For instance, '*Man* is living' then has the form

.3 $Cl[\![a]\!] \in \subset [\![b]\!]$

(definitions II §5.19, §5.17, §5.18 refer). Now .3 represents an inclusion which, given that it involves quasi-names, is an analogue of a true exemplification of sentences having the '*a* ∈ *b*' form, wherein the '∈' is the primitive 'is' of Ontology (II §2.211). The use of 'Cl[ ]' for the first argument of the '∈' of .3 ensures that there is exactly one species of the *a*'s in question, for from II §5.24 we have:

.4 $[a] : [\exists \varphi] . Cl[\![a]\!] \in \varphi$

which is isomorphic with the *definiens* of the lower-order 'There exists exactly one . . .' ('ob( )', II §4.3.3). At the same time the use of '⊂[ ]' as the second argument of the '∈' of .3 ensures that the *a*'s and the *b*'s need not be co-extensive; other species may be included among the *b*'s. These properties, it may be noted, run parallel to the truth-conditions for the primitive, name-flanked, '∈' (II §2.211).

The way is now open to the provision of an unproblematic analysis of William of Sherwood's intentions. It has already been noted above that his notion of the *common* (numerical) division of the subject by 'Every' amounts to the *descensus* used by Ockham for the elucidation of 'Every *a* is *b*', i.e.

.5 $[ab] : a \sqsubset b . \supset . x_1 \cap a \in b . x_2 \cap a \in b . x_3 \cap a \in b \dots$

(cf. §1.12). Without any further ado one may immediately conjecture, in view of the analogies between the two levels of '∈' and their arguments noted in the last paragraph, that the higher-order version of the consequent of .5, with its units modelled on the general form of .3, will serve to represent those intentions, i.e. the *proper* (specific) division effected by 'Every' in 'every *a* is *b*' is shown in the following:

.6 $Cl[\![x_1 \cap a]\!] \in \subset [\![b]\!] . Cl[\![x_2 \cap a]\!] \in \subset [\![b]\!] .$
          $Cl[\![x_3 \cap a]\!] \in \subset [\![b]\!] \dots$

Thus in the case which has hitherto served as an example in our considerations, i.e. 'Every animal is living', wherein the *animal* has to be divided into its several sub-species, the subscripted *x* now has to be taken as a given species-name, and *animal* and *living* are the instances of *a* and *b*. Typical units of .6 would then be '*Elephant-animal* is *living*' '*Man-animal* is *living*', '*Giraffe-animal* is *living*', and so on, with the italicisation as a crude indication that the arguments of the 'is' are those appropriate to a higher-order 'is' at the level of species-talk (cf. II §5.19). Reference to the definitions involved (cf. .3 above) makes it evident that .6, unlike the consequent of .5, has *no* existential import, exactly as required in this case.

That the whole conjecture just described is not only intuitively, but also deductively, connected with .5, will be proved below. In the meantime, however, it turns out to have the unsuspected bonus of resolving a difficult point of interpretation in William's text. This arises when his example is one such as 'Every man is animal', the subject (man) of which has no obvious sub-species ('specific' or 'proximate' parts) into which 'Every' can divide it when a *proper* division of that subject is in question. His words which cover such divisions under those circumstances are mysteriously opaque:

.7   . . . a specific part is a part that is due to a universal insofar as it is a universal— i.e. a part in the sense that it is a conditionally extant [part]. A numerical part, on the other hand, is an actually extant part, not due to a universal as such. A part of man in the first sense is man conditionally in Socrates; likewise man conditionally in Plato. Even if no man actually exists, these parts are. A part of man in the second sense is man actually in Socrates, or Socrates; likewise man actually in Plato. Unless there is an actually existing man, these parts are not.

(*WSS* 20)

. . . *pars secundum speciem est pars quae debetur universali in quantum est universale, et haec est pars secundum quod est habitualiter ens. Pars autem secundum numerum est pars actualiter ens et non debetur universali per se. Primo modo pars hominis est homo habitualiter in Sorte . . . et similiter homo habitualiter in Platone, et hae partes sunt nullo homine actualiter existente. Secundo modo est pars hominis actualiter in Sorte . . . et similiter homo actualiter in Platone, et hae partes non sunt nisi homine actualiter existente.*

(*WST* 49)

Now the segments of this text which refer to *common* division into numerical parts are plain enough, and are obviously covered by .5. However, when treating of *proper* division into specific parts, we have the *homo habitualiter in Sorte* which *WSS* translates as 'man conditionally in Socrates', as an indication of one of these specific parts. How is it possible to understand this non-existential unit? In fact, the use of .6, but with a reversion to the interpretation of the subscripted x formerly proper to .5 (cf. §1.12), yields all that is required. In other words, cases such as that of *man* wherein (according to the medievals) there are none of the appropriate sub-species as there were in the case of *animal*, require that with 'man' for the 'a''s of .6, the subscripted 'x''s of .6 must be taken to be either proper names of the usual sort, if available (e.g. 'Socrates', 'Plato', etc.) or instances of the ambiguous proper name 'this'; in both cases the names must be such as apply to human beings. Under these circumstances one still has a conjunction of units at the 'specific' (higher-order '$\in$') level, none of which has existential import, unlike the units of the consequence of .5.

Not only does this conjecture actually fit the requirements of the case in the way outlined; it can also be proved to be deductively connected with .5. Hence if William accepts .5, then he not only may accept .6 as a further consequent of .5, but is in fact committed to it. Here now is a proof of the connection in question. First, some preliminary theses of Ontology are needed:

.8 $[a] . a \circ a$ (II §5.14)
.9 $[ab] : a \in b . \supset . a \subset b$ (II §5.9)
.10 $[abc] : \mathrm{Cl}[\![a]\!] (b) . \mathrm{Cl}[\![a]\!] (c) . \supset . b \circ c$ (II §4.3.12, II §4.3.18)

One may then show that any one of the units of the consequent of .5 implies the corresponding unit of .6 by the use of the thesis now to be proved:

.11 $[ab] : a \in b . \supset . \mathrm{Cl}[\![a]\!] \in \subset [\![b]\!]$
      $[ab] ::$
         (1) $a \in b . \supset :.$
         (2) $a \circ a .$ (.8)
         (3) $a \subset b .$ (1, .9)
         (4) $\mathrm{Cl}[\![a]\!] (a) .$ (II §5.18, 2)
         (5) $\subset [\![b]\!] (a) :$ (II §5.17, 3)
         (6) $[\exists c] . \mathrm{Cl}[\![a]\!] (c) . \subset [\![b]\!] (c) :.$ (4, 5)
         (7) $[de] : \mathrm{Cl}[\![a]\!] (d) . \mathrm{Cl}[\![a]\!] (e) . \supset . d \circ e :.$ (.10)
             $\mathrm{Cl}[\![a]\!] \in \subset [\![b]\!]$ (II §5.19, 6, 7)

From .11, with '$x_1 \cap a$' substituted for its 'a', one has '$\mathrm{Cl}[\![x_1 \cap a]\!] \in \subset [\![b]\!]$' as the consequence of the '$x_1 \cap a \in b$' unit of the consequent of .5, and so on for the other units, as shown in .6.

In short, the Ontological analysis of a unit of William's 'specific' division (as in .3), coupled with the acceptance of an Ockham-type *descensus* elucidation of his 'numerical' division (.5), has thrown light on a way of interpreting that specific division (as in .6) capable of coping with one of its problematic instances, namely that which occurs when individual names are involved in what is nevertheless a non-existential division of a species having no sub-species. This illustrates the suggestive power contained in the medieval material undergoing examination; that material itself has directed the course of the investigation, and inspired deductions such as .8 to .11 above.

However, the starting point of the deductions performed above was .5, with its existential strong inclusion ('$\sqsubset$'), whereas William's specific division (.6) would appear to be intended as the consequence of a non-existential weak inclusion ('$\subset$'). We now show, in .14 below, that the weak inclusion does in fact imply an expression of which the specific division (.6) is an instance. The proof of .12, on which .14 in part depends, is almost identical with that of .11, and hence need not be stated in full.

.12 $[ab] : a \subset b . \supset . \text{Cl}[\![a]\!] \in \subset [\![b]\!]$ (II §5.17, §5.18, §5.19, .8, .10)

.13 $[ab] : a \subset b . \supset . [c] . c \cap a \subset b$
     $[ab] :: $
       (1) $a \subset b . \supset :.$
       (2) $[d] : d \in a . \supset . d \in b :.$ (II §4.3.5, 1)
       (3) $[dc] : d \in a . d \in c . \supset . d \in b :.$ (2)
        $[c] . c \cap a \subset b$ (§1.7, II §4.3.5, 3)

.14 $[ab] : a \subset b . \supset . [c] . \text{Cl}[\![c \cap a]\!] \in \subset [\![b]\!]$ (.12, .13)

Thus far we are dealing with theses of Ontology. We now turn to the instances of .14 which are generated by using 'x_1', 'x_2', 'x_3', etc. as successive substituends for the 'c' of .14. The intervention of these constant terms hence yields:

.15 $[ab] : a \subset b . \supset . \text{Cl}[\![x_1 \cap a]\!] \in \subset [\![b]\!] . \text{Cl}[\![x_2 \cap a]\!] \in \subset [\![b]\!] .$
     $\text{Cl}[\![x_3 \cap a]\!] \in \subset [\![b]\!] \ldots .$

If the 'x'-substituends are taken to be species-names relative to 'a' as a genus-name, then one has the non-existential division into species, as described above. If, however, 'b' is itself a species-name, leaving only individuals to be its 'parts', then one still has a non-existential division with the 'x'-substituends now names of 'conditionally extent' individuals, as required by William.

Unfortunately, although we have now apparently satisfied William's requirements by means of the analysis proposed above, a sophism which he claims to solve by reference to the distinction between specific and numerical division is not in fact susceptible of such a solution. Thus, relative to the supposition that there are only asses, he claims that 'Every animal is an ass, and every man is an animal, therefore every man is an ass' is fallacious, and that the fallacy is resoluble by means of the distinction now in question (*WSS* 21). In point of fact, contrary to his assertions, if the three inclusions in this inference are taken specifically (cf. 15), then the inference is valid and all three are true just because there are no men. Again, he is wrong in supposing that a conclusion does not follow from the first taken numerically (cf. .5) and the second taken specifically (cf. .15); the conclusion will follow and be true in its specific sense (cf. .15), once again just because there are no men. He is only right in claiming that if the first is taken numerically (cf. .5) it is true, while the second taken numerically (cf. 5.) is false, so that this combination falls from consideration. Of course, further complications in the analyses of the two sorts of division might save his account of the sophism, but it would appear more reasonable to surmise that that account involves errors stemming from the complexity of the functors involved and from his lack of a means of resolving that complexity into simple elements of the sort available to us.

§4   NEGATION AND NON-BEING

In the foregoing sections the advantages of not being confined to restricted quantification and to forms such as '$\varphi(x)$' for the purpose of analysis of medieval themes has been readily apparent. These advantages become even more salient when problems concerning negation and non-being are broached (cf. II §2.2521 and the close of II §4.3). If we remain within the bounds of the '$\varphi(x)$' sort of form, then its negation '$\sim (\varphi(x))$' has to do duty for what it may sometimes be useful to distinguish as two differing cases. Thus one may want to distinguish between such a negation's being true because the x in question is a non-φ-er, and its being true because the x just does not exist. For example 'This table is not a horse' could be described as being true for the first reason, whereas 'Pegasus is not a philosopher' is true for the second. However, the use of restricted quantification (II §2.25) operates as a compensatory mechanism which, by its non-admission of empty names as substituends for nominal variables, removes the second case from the field of situations coverable by '$\sim (\varphi(x))$'. It therefore so happens that '$\sim (\varphi(x))$', involving as it does the propositional negation '$\sim$' turns out to be coincidentally adequate for the expression of the forms of propositions whose inner structures may for certain purposes be better detailed by an analysis of the form '*x* is a non-φ-er', wherein the 'non-φ-er' represents the negation of a nominal form rather than the negation of a propositional form. This coincidental adequacy subsists until the difficulties of empty definite descriptions standing in the place of '*x*' arise, e.g. if 'The present king of France is not bald' is in question. In the face of such difficulties the distinction which has evidently been desirable all along is introduced in a tortuous and *ad hoc* fashion under the misleading guise of the 'primary and secondary occurrence' of descriptions (*RI* 179) and all names have to be construed as disguised descriptions in order to be able to take advantage of this *ad hoc* distinction.

Now it is clearly advantageous to avoid a system whose compensatory defects enable one to gloss over nominal negation by the use of propositional negation in the inefficient manner described. Let the plain commonsense fact therefore be restated, namely that one may wish to distinguish between *two* reasons why '$\sim (\varphi(x))$' may hold: (i) because although *x* exists, it is a non-φ-er, and (ii) because *x* does not exist and so is not anything at all. Now the medievals, following Aristotle and Boethius (cf. *HDG* §6.3421), were familiar enough with the distinction between the case in which a *name* is negated (required for the expression of reason (i)) and the case in which a *proposition* is negated (which may occur for *both* of the reasons mentioned). The first case, that of the nominal negation ('N ( )'), is catered for by definition II §4.3.15, repeated at .3 below, and the second by propositional negation ('$\sim$') introduced informally at II §3.1.5. Walter Burleigh, the fourteenth-century medieval logician whose work in this direction is shortly to be discussed, is conscious of this distinction, and aware that a proposition having the form '*a* is *b*' may not be the case simply because the *a* in question does not exist. He therefore adds a clause stating the existence of *a* when a premiss of the type of 'It is not the case that *a* is *b*' is being used, as in the example of 'It is not the case that Socrates is a white log', reproduced below.

Nevertheless, in the absence of a precise artificial language, errors and imprecisions can all too easily enter into an otherwise intuitively acute treatment and use of negation. This is especially so when nominal negation is used in respect of what were known as 'transcendental' terms such as *ens* 'being', *res* 'thing', and *aliquid* 'something'. A few reminders of definitions and theorems which ensue therefrom will provide coordinates in terms of which may be measured both the acuteness and the imprecisions of St Anselm and of Walter Burleigh in this respect:

.1	$[a] : a \in \wedge . \equiv . a \in a . \sim (a \in a)$	(II §4.3.14)
.2	$[a] : a \in \vee . \equiv . a \in a$	(II §4.3.13)
.3	$[a] : a \in N(b) . \equiv . a \in a . \sim (a \in b)$	(II §4.3.15)

.4 $[a] : a \in \wedge . \supset . a \in N(v)$
$[a] : .$
   (1) $a \in \wedge . \supset :$
   (2) $a \in a . \sim (a \in a) :$ (.1, 1)
   (3) $a \in a . \sim (a \in v) :$ (.2, 2)
       $a \in N(v)$ (.3, 3)

.5 $[a] : a \in N(v) . \supset . a \in \wedge$
$[a] : .$
   (1) $a \in N(v) . \supset :$
   (2) $a \in a . \sim (a \in v) :$ (.3, 1)
   (3) $\sim (a \in a) :$ (.2, 2)
       $a \in \wedge$ (.1, 3)

.6 $\wedge \circ N(v)$ (.4, .5, II §4.3.12)
.7 $[a] . \sim (a \in \wedge)$ (.1)
.8 $[ab] : a \in a . \sim (a \in b) . \supset . [\exists c] . a \in N(c)$ (.3)

The Latin *non* may normally be translated sometimes as 'not' and sometimes as the prefix 'non-' (as in 'non-white'). However, in order to reflect the nature of the original Latin, which lacks this distinction, *non* will hereunder be invariably translated by 'not'. Further, the assumption that 'v' (cf. .2 above) may serve as the counterpart of *ens* 'being' or *aliquid* 'something', at least for present purposes, will be adopted. The definitions and theses given above evidently carry with them the further assumption that problem-sentences involving words like *nihil* 'nothing' and *aliquid* 'something' which grammatically are nominal in character may sometimes be analysed in such a fashion that this nominal character need not be totally dissolved away in favour of arrangements of quantifiers. It will become evident below that both Anselm and Burleigh held that *nihil* 'nothing' sometimes has to be parsed as an empty name and sometimes has to be represented as not being a name at all, but rather as performing a logical function for the representation of which only the quantificational parts of logical sentences are appropriate. Ontology enables one to concur in this duality of opinion, contrary to what would be the case in most other current systems of logic (cf. *HL* §6.641) and hence has the capacity to follow Burleigh's employment of *both* approaches within a single sentence, as in the 'Nothing is nothing' case mentioned below.

First Anselm's appreciation of the distinction between nominal negation (.3) and propositional negation ('~') may be approached by way of a discussion which occurs in his *De Grammatico*:

.9   STUDENT. *White* signifies   DISCIPULUS. *Albus aut*
        either *something* having   *aliquid significat habens*

whiteness or it signifies *nothing*. But *nothing* cannot be understood as having whiteness. Hence *white* must signify something having whiteness.

albedinem aut nihil. Sed nihil non potest intelligi habens albedinem. Necesse est ergo ut albus significet aliquid habens albedinem.

TUTOR. When it is asserted that *white* signifies either *something* having whiteness or *nothing*, and this is interpreted as asserting that *white* signifies either *something having* or *not-something having*, then as *not-something* is an infinite name, this disjunction is neither complete nor true, and hence proves nothing. It's like asserting 'The blind man either sees *something* or he sees *not-something*'. If, on the other hand, the assertion is interpreted as meaning that the word either signifies or does not signify *something having*, the disjunction is complete and true. . . .

MAGISTER. *Si quis autem dicit quia albus aut aliquid significat habens albedinem aut nihil: si sic intelligitur ac si diceretur: albus aut significat aliquid habens aut significat non-aliquid habens, ut non-aliquid sit infinitum nomen, non est integra nec vera divisio, et ideo nihil probat. Veluti si quis diceret, Caecus aut videt aliquid aut videt non-aliquid. Si vero sic intelligitur, quia aut significat aliquid habens aut non significat: integra est divisio et vera.*

(*HDG* 4.8021, 4.813)

The elucidation here given by the Tutor is sufficient to make the point. The presupposed equation of *nihil* 'nothing' with *non-aliquid* 'not-something' enables one to see the Student's assertion that *white* either signifies something having whiteness or nothing as involving the disjunction of two quasi-*nominal* forms, one positive and the other negative ('something' and 'not-something') rather than the disjunction of two *propositions*, one positive and the other negative, as required by the Principle of the Excluded Middle (i.e. $[p] \cdot p \vee \sim p$). One of the nominal forms in question, namely 'not-something', is termed an 'infinite name' by the Tutor—a characterisation which makes clear that we are concerned with nominal negation of the sort defined at .3 above, rather than with propositional negation. For Boethius and the medievals an infinite name, roughly speaking, was a shared name with the prefix '*non-*' added to it; this may be gathered from *B* 304D,

424D, 764D, 795D and 882A–B. The passage quoted above shows
that Anselm well realises how a disjunction constituted with the help
of a name and its negation (as in 'The blind man either sees something
or he sees not-something' or 'The present king of France is a father
or the present king of France is childless') does not yield a truth, since
it is not exhaustive of the possibilities of the situation (*non est integra
nec vera divisio*). What is wanted is the disjunction of a proposition
and its negation, as in 'Either the blind man sees something or it is
not the case that the blind man sees something'. We then have a true
exemplification of the Principle of the Excluded Middle.

Anselm's treatment of the problem of non-being and nothingness
again presupposes the already-mentioned equation of *nihil* 'nothing'
with *non-aliquid* 'not-something', and in the passage which now
follows, the ambiguity of the latter is plainly causing trouble:

.10   In like fashion *blindness* is
said to be *something*, if we
go by the form of speech
employed, when from the
point of view of how things
are it is *not something*. For
we say that someone has
sight, and that sight is in
them, in exactly the same
fashion as we say that
someone has blindness, and
that blindness is in them,
when the latter is not *something*, but rather *nothing*,
and the 'having' here in
question is not the having of
something, but rather the
lacking of that which is
something. For blindness is
just non-sightedness, or the
absence of sight where sight
ought to be. But of course
non-sight or the absence of
sight is no more *something*
in a situation where sight
should be than in one where
it ought not to be. Hence
blindness is no more *something* with reference to the

*Ita quoque caecitas dicitur
aliquid secundum formam
loquendi, cum non sit aliquid
secundum rem. Sicut enim de
aliquo dicimus quia habet
visum et visus est in eo:
ita dicimus quia habet
caecitatem, et caecitas est in
eo, cum haec non sit aliquid
sed potius non-aliquid: et
hanc habere non sit aliquid
habere, immo eo carere quod
est aliquid. Caecitas namque
non est aliud quam non-visus
aut absentia visus ubi visus
debet esse. Non visus vero
vel absentia visus non magis
est aliquid ubi debet esse
visus, quam ubi non debet
esse. Quare caecitas non
magis est aliquid in oculo
quia ibi debet esse visus,
quam non-visus vel absentia
visus in lapide ubi visus non
debet esse. Multa quoque alia
similiter dicuntur aliquid
secundum formam loquendi
quae non sunt aliquid,
quoniam sic loquimur de illis*

eye (wherein sight is properly to be found) than non-
sight or the absence of sight
is *something* in a stone (sight
not being proper to a stone).
Many other things are
likewise said to be *something* (if we go by the form
of utterance) whereas they
are *not something*: we just
speak about them in the
same way as we speak about
existing things. It is in this
sort of way, then, that 'evil'
and 'nothing' signify *something*: that which is signified
is *not something* from the
point of view of how things
are, but only if we go by the
form of expression used.
'Nothing' signifies just *not-
something*, or the absence of
those things that are *something*.

*sicut de rebus existentibus.
Hoc igitur modo 'malum' et
'nihil' significant aliquid; et
quod significatur est aliquid
non secundum rem, sed
secundum formam loquendi.
'Nihil' enim non aliud
significat quam non-aliquid,
aut absentia eorum quae sunt
aliquid.*

(*De Casu Diaboli* 11, *HL* 214–5)

Anselm is here making an important point, namely the distinction
between the merely grammatical form and the real or logical form
of an utterance. This is, however, not our primary concern. (For
further details see *HL* §6.65.) Our present focus of interest lies in the
equation of a term denoting a privation, namely 'blind(ness)', with
an infinite name, i.e. 'not-sighted(ness)', and the consequent inference
in the light of the equation recalled before .10 that a privation is a
nothing. Crudely speaking, our aim now is to check on whether all
not-somethings are thus really cases of *nothing*, as Anselm appears to
hold.

Doubt may first of all be cast on this apparent Anselmian contention
by assuming that all infinite names (including those corresponding
to privations) are instances of the '*N*( )' defined at .3 above. Next
one may distinguish between two sorts of infinite name: there are
those in which the argument which completes '*N*( )' is a non-empty
name other than 'v' and its natural-language counterparts such as
the transcendentals; with these may be contrasted those infinite names
in which 'v' or some one or other of its natural-language counterparts

stands as completion of the '*n*( )'. In the second event we have a nominal form which, as will be shown in a moment, may justly be equated with 'nothing', whereas this is not so in the first case. As we have seen, Anselm slips from the first to the second by insisting that non-sighted(ness) is a *non-aliquid* 'not-something', and then uses the latter (*via* the equation recorded before .10 above) to yield *nothing* as a characterisation of non-sighted(ness).

In fact, the ambiguity of 'not-something' (*non-aliquid*) leaps to the eye when the situation of expressions of the form '*a* is not-something' ('*a* ∈ *n*( )') within the field of our definitions and theorems is recalled. From .6 and .7 we have:

.11   [*a*] . ~ (*a* ∈ *n*(v))

In this case, as remarked above, '*n*(v)' as the instance of '*n*( )' yields a sense of 'not-something' which may rightly be construed as being the equivalent of 'nothing'. As .11 reminds us, it is *never* the case that anything *is* not-something in this sense. On the other hand, if the something undergoing the negation is represented by a non-transcendental term, as in 'not-sighted', 'not-man', and so on, then as .8 shows, it only needs a couple of often-fulfilled conditions for the consequence to ensue that an object *is* a not-something of this sort, and hence certainly not a nothing. I may be a non-table, but I am not on that account a nothing. Thus, although it is in a general way true that both infinite names and *nihil* 'nothing' can be said to involve *non-aliquid* 'not-something', as Anselm holds, the two different sorts of 'something' which can be affected by the nominal negation make a whole world of difference to the precise sense of *non-aliquid* 'not-something'. Only the sense illustrated by the second argument of the '∈' of .11 really amounts to *nihil* 'nothing'.

Turning now to Burleigh we find that the section on negation in his *De Puritate Artis Logicae* treats most competently the whole range of topics so far mooted. Thus first of all we have the distinction between propositional negation and nominal negation:

.12   It should therefore be realised that the negation 'not' can be taken either merely negatively or infinitively. When it is taken merely negatively, then it always negates some propositional complex or something which is essential to the structure of the

Sciendum ergo, quod haec negatio 'non' potest teneri mere negative vel infinitive. Quando tenetur mere negative, tunc semper negat aliquam compositionem vel aliquid quod est formale in propositione. Sed quando tenetur infinitive, tunc negat aliquod extremum in

proposition. But when it is taken infinitively, then it negates some nominal element (*extremum*) in the proposition, namely the subject or predicate. First, therefore, we discuss the word 'not' in so far as it is taken merely negatively, as well as some other things which comprise the merely negative. Then we can discuss some points about the same expression in so far as it is taken infinitively.

propositione, scilicet subiectum vel praedicatum. Primo igitur dicamus de haec dictio 'non' ut tenetur mere negative et de quibusdam aliis quae meram negationem includunt, et deinde dicemus aliqua de de ipsa ut tenetur infinitive.

(*BDP* 223.1.8)

Burleigh then goes on to deal with a 'sophisma'—a problem-sentence or problem-inference—in the light of the fact that the point of impingement of a negation can be ambiguous when it affects a complex expression. It may be noted that it is the *nominal* and not the *propositional* negation which is mistakenly used in the production of the sophistical counterproof stated below. In that counterproof it is quite overtly stated that 'not-something' is equatable with 'nothing'. The translation has been accordingly angled in order to produce the full flavour of the 'not-something' effect which is to be found in the original Latin:

.13   It should therefore be realised that the following is a rule: whenever the word 'not' modifies an expression involving many elements, then the result is a complex expression, since the negation 'not' can negate one or other of the elements modified.

It is on the basis of this rule that the following sophisma may be solved:

Not something is what you are and you are a donkey

Sciendum ergo pro regula, quod quandocumque haec dictio 'non' ponitur in oratione cum multis determinabilibus est oratio multiplex, ex eo quod haec negatio 'non' potest negare unum istorum deter-minabilium vel alterum.

Et per hoc solvitur hoc sophisma:

Non aliquid es et tu es asinus Probatur sic: 'Aliquid es et tu es asinus', haec est falsa; ergo haec est vera: 'Non aliquid es et tu es asinus'.

Proof: 'Something is what you are and you are a donkey' is false, hence the following is true: 'Not something is what you are and you are a donkey'. Counterproof: In 'Not something is what you are and you are a donkey' the 'not-something' is equivalent to 'nothing': whence 'Nothing is what you are and you are a donkey', which is false.

Solution: The first proposition is ambiguous, in that the 'not' can either negate the 'is' which occurs first, in which case the proposition is false, since it amounts to the following conjunctive proposition:

No thing is what you are
  and you are a donkey

Or it may negate the sign of conjunction, in which case it is true and

(a) denotes that the following conjunctive proposition is not true: 'Something is what you are and you are a donkey',

(b) is then equivalent to the following disjunctive proposition: 'Either nothing is what you are or it's not the case that you are a donkey.'

Improbatur sic: Non aliquid es et tu es asinus. 'Non aliquid' et 'nihil' aequipollent, ergo nihil es et tu es asinus, quod est falsum. Solutio. Prima est multiplex, ex eo quod haec negatio 'non' potest negare hoc verbum 'est' primo loco positum, et sic est falsa, quia valet istam copulativum: 'Nihil es et tu es asinus'. Vel potest negare notam copulationis, et sic est vera et denotatur quod haec copulativa non est vera: 'Aliquid es et tu es asinus' et tunc aequipollet huic disiunctivae: 'Nihil es vel tu non es asinus'.

(*BDP* 223.8.25)

The 'Proof' part of this passage simply takes a false conjunctive proposition of the form '$p . q$' and adds the negation 'not' to the whole thing. In other words, '$\sim (p . q)$' is the form of the true proposition intended, with the 'not' representing propositional negation. In the 'Counterproof', however, this 'not' is taken to be nominal negation

('N( )') and is combined with the immediately-following 'something' to produce 'not-something', i.e. 'nothing', if we use the Anselmian type of equation noted above. The true proposition which could have emerged from the 'Proof' is hence now being parsed so as to appear a false conjunction consisting of two false conjuncts. In the 'Solution', however, Burleigh rightly insists on tracing the trouble with the original proposition to the possibility of misplaced use of propositional negation. According to him the initial 'not' can be taken either to negate the first conjunct (in which case the original proposition becomes false as a whole since it now has two false conjuncts) or to negate the conjunction as a whole. In the latter case, by the thesis:

.14 $[pq] : \sim (p \cdot q) \cdot \equiv \cdot \sim p \vee \sim q$

one has the true disjunction of two negations, the first of which ('It is not the case that something is what you are') is worked out as 'Nothing is what you are'. It is the second of these negations, i.e. 'It is not the case that you are a donkey', which makes the whole disjunction true.

We now pass directly to Burleigh's treatment of nominal negation, i.e. the 'N( )' of .3 above:

.15   In brief, for the infinite negation of an expression four conditions must be fulfilled:

         First, that that expression which it is required to negate infinitively should signify some finite thing;

         Second, that the addition of the infinitising negation should be totally remotive of the import of that expression;

         Third, that the infinitising negation should leave or permit alternative structures (*alias naturas*). Hence an infinitising negation should not be remotive of *all* structures, but only of the structure implied by the expression to which it is added . . .;

Breviter ad hoc quod aliqua dictio infinitetur, requiruntur quatuor conditiones.

Prima, quod illa dictio quae debet infinitari, significet aliquam rem finitam.

Secunda conditio, quod negatio infinitans addita illi dictioni, importata per istam dictionem destruat.

Tertia conditio, quod illa negatio infinitans alias naturas derelinquat seu permittat. Unde negatio infinitans non debet omnem naturam destruere, sed solum naturam importam per dictionem cui additur . . .

Fourth; that the term which it is required to negate infinitely should be simple and not composed of substantive and adjective or of adjectives. This is because that which has to be infinitely negated must be a unity, whereas a term composed as described is not strictly one. Hence the term 'log which is white' cannot be infinitely negated; and if a negation is prefixed which yields 'Not log which is white' then nothing is infinitely negated save the term 'log'.

It results from the *first* condition that syncategorematic terms cannot be infinitely negated, since they have no finite signification.

It results from the *second* condition that an infinite name differs from a privative one, since a privative name is not altogether remotive of the structure of that with which it is conjoined, but rather shows removal of the structure while retaining the thing structured, so that *blindness* is remotive of *sight* but retains *eye*. An infinitising negation does not retain the subject of the structure removed by the infinitising negation.

It results from the *third* condition that transcendental names cannot be infinitely negated, since were they to be thus negated,

Quarta conditio est quod terminus qui debet infinitari, sit simplex et non compositus ex substantivo et adiectivo nec ex adiectivis. Illud enim quod debet infinitari, debet esse unum: sed terminus talis aggregatus non est simpliciter unus. Unde ille terminus 'lignum album' non potest infinitari; et si addatur negatio dicendo 'non lignum album' nihil infitatur nisi iste terminus 'lignum'.

Propter primam conditionem syncategoremata non possunt infinitari, quia non important significationem finitam.

Propter secundam conditionem differt nomen infinitum a nomine privativo, quia terminus privativus non destruit omnino naturam illius cui additur, sed destruit formam et ponit subiectum formae, ut 'caecitas' destruit visum et ponit oculum: sed negatio infinitans non ponit subiectum formae destructae per negationem infinitantem.

Propter tertiam conditionem non possunt nomina transcendentia infinitari, quia si infinitarentur, nulla natura

7

there would remain no sort of structure of which the resulting name could be predicated. Hence, were 'not-being' an infinite name, it could not be asserted of any being; this, however, does not agree with the notion of the infinite term, for an infinite term should be assertible of some existent. This is why I lay it down that 'being' taken in its widest extent cannot be infinitely negated and does not have any contradictory apart from a purely verbal one.

relinqueretur, de qua possent dici. Unde si 'non ens' esset terminus infinitus, non posset de aliquo ente dici, et hoc est contra rationem termini infiniti: nam terminus infinitus debet dici de ente. Et ideo dico quod 'ens' in sua maxima communitate non potest infinitari nec habet contradictorium nisi secundum vocem.

It results from the *fourth* condition that the following is not valid:

Socrates is not a white log and Socrates exists,
Hence Socrates is a not-white log.

This invalidity arises because the whole term is not negated in the conclusion, but only the word 'white'.

Propter quartem conditionem non sequitur: Sortes non est album lignum, et Sortes est, ergo Sortes est non album lignum, quia in consequente non infinitatur totum sed solum li 'album'.
(*BDP* 231.27–232.24)

Although Burleigh himself doubtless sees his distinction between infinite and privative names as one of the important results of this passage, from the point of view of the present investigation both types of name are of interest only in so far as they exemplify nominal negation. For our part the main point which emerges from the passage is that Burleigh has here at least the means whereby to differentiate between the two senses of *non-aliquid* 'not-something' which (as we saw above) Anselm apparently failed to distinguish.

It is in his statement of the results of the third condition that Burleigh shows himself to be quite conscious of the special properties of *non-ens* 'not-being' (i.e. '*N*(v)') which is in fact that sense of *non-aliquid* 'not-something' which can correctly be equated with the nominal *nihil* 'nothing'. Thus, as Burleigh says, were 'non-being' (in

the sense indicated) an infinite name, it could not (truly) be asserted
of any subject. This is in fact his expression of exactly the point of
.11 above. Unfortunately he takes this as evidence that *non-ens* 'not-
being' is not really an infinite name, his presupposition being at this
point that all names must name something. (We have already seen
that St Anselm does not share this presupposition.) However, it is
quite evident from .11 and its predecessors that there is no reason
why this should be so. The non-metalinguistic version of the point
he is making is simply that no object is a non-entity; there would thus
appear to be no reason why 'non-being' should not at least be *denied*
of a subject. Strangely enough, although at this point Burleigh appears
to be working in terms of this doctrine that all names, and hence
infinite names too, must name something, he nevertheless is not working in these terms in the example of the white log wherein the proper
name 'Socrates' figures. Otherwise he would not have had to add the
existence-clause which appears in that example, i.e. 'Socrates exists'.
Nevertheless it is quite evident that he does realise that there is a
difference between *non ens* 'not being' and other negated names.
Thesis .11 above is the modern counterpart of this realisation, with
.8 laying down the conditions which constitute the contrast in the case
of other negated names.

Finally there is the fourth condition (cf. *HL* §3.12231) and its results.
Of course, if we wish to negate a compound name-like expression such
as 'white log', then it is a mistake to suppose, as Burleigh supposes,
that the prefixing of the negation to the compound merely negates
the first member of that compound (yielding 'not-white log'). Now
Burleigh has in fact shown himself to be well aware of the analogous
point in propositional contexts, as the end of the first of his passages
quoted above (.13) amply demonstrates. There he rightly takes the
negation of a conjunctive *proposition* to consist of the disjunction of
the negated conjuncts (cf. .14 above). It is a pity that he now does not
appear to realise that the negation of a conjunctive *term* can likewise
be taken to consist of the disjunction of the negated conjuncts. Hence,
rather than putting a veto on the negation of conjunctive terms, he
should have read such a negation as 'either not-*a* or not-*b*'. The
conclusion of the final inference which he depicts as invalid should
hence read 'Socrates is either not-white or not-log', which is true
because of the second disjunct, reminding us as it does that Socrates
is a non-log. (§1.7 defines a nominal conjunction of the sort which
would serve here. §1.8 shows a nominal disjunction which, along
with nominal negation, could show the form of this last conclusion.)

In connection with the topic which first launched us into this
section, Burleigh has at least realised that in an inference such as this
final one, wherein the negation of a form representable by '*a* is *b*' is

posited, the addition of a clause to the effect that *a* exists is necessary if one desires to cut out the possibility of the negation's being true merely on account of the non-existence of the proposition's subject. This then leaves the negation of the second term ('*b*') as the reason for the negation of the whole sentence. Burleigh realises this also, his only failure being the lack of the ability to carry through this negation correctly when a conjunctive term is involved, as we have just seen.

Thus far our attention has been concentrated on examples in which 'nothing' and cognate terms were representable by recourse to nominal forms such as '∧' and 'ɴ(∨)'. As already mentioned, however, medieval authors were aware of the alternative way of construing 'nothing' by the use of quantifiers—a way which is the only one available in the more familiar systems of contemporary logic, with their restricted quantification. Thus Anselm distinguishes between the two cases in *Monologion* 19 by recourse to the ingenious example, *Nihil me docuit volare* 'Nothing taught me to fly'. He in effect points out that if 'nothing' is here construed as a name, then the sentence is false. However, if by recourse to the equation between *nihil* 'nothing' and *non-aliquid* 'not-something' one splits up the 'nothing' into '(it's) not (that) something . . .', yielding '(It's) not (that) something taught me to fly', or in Latin *Non me docuit aliquid volare*, then the result is a true sentence (cf. *HL* §6.66). It is obvious that this last occurrence of '(It's) not (that) something . . .' corresponds fairly closely to the '∼([∃*x*] . . .)' which would nowadays be the standard and correct fashion of analysing 'nothing' as it occurs in Anselm's sentence.

Burleigh's efforts in this direction are more complex, and are of interest in so far as they involve the introduction of sentences wherein both sorts of treatment, the nominal and the quantificational, are mingled. Thus Burleigh asserts:

.16 | Whenever two universal negative signs are placed in some expression, the first is equivalent to its contrary, and the second to its contradictory. By reference to this rule the following sophisma may be resolved:
Nothing is nothing.
This may be proved thus: its contradictory, namely 'Something is nothing' is false, hence the following is true, namely 'Nothing is | *Quandocumque in aliqua locutione ponuntur duo signa universalia negativa, primum aequipollet suo contrario, secundum suo contradictorio. Et per hoc solvitur hoc sophisma:*
  Nihil est nihil.
Probatur sic: Sua contradictoria est falsa: '*Aliquid est nihil*', *ergo haec est vera:* '*Nihil est nihil*' . . .
Solutio. Prima vera est, quia aequipollet huic: '*Quodlibet*

nothing' ...
    Solution: the first proposition *is* true, but this is because it is equivalent to 'Anything you please is something', which is true. This may now be shown: 'Nothing' is the same as 'anything you please not ...'. Hence to assert 'Nothing is nothing' is the same as to assert 'Anything you please is not nothing'. This in turn amounts to 'Anything you please is something'.

est aliquid', quae vera est; quod apparet. Nam 'nihil' idem est quod 'quodlibet non'; idem ergo est dicere: 'Nihil nihil est' et dicere: 'Quodlibet non nihil est'. Valet istam: 'Quodlibet est aliquid'.
                              (*BDP* 226.33–227.13)

This short passage contains a wealth of highly interesting material. In the first place the key to the solution given lies, according to Burleigh, in the allegedly general rule stated at the beginning of the passage. For him 'anything you please' (*quodlibet*) is the contrary of 'nothing', and 'something' is the latter's contradictory in the sense that one or other of '. . . is nothing' and '. . . is something' must hold of any *x*. (Note the resemblance between this and the Student's point in passage .9 above.) Hence by recourse to the allegedly general rule stated, 'Nothing is nothing' becomes 'Anything you please is something'.

From our point of view, however, the interest of this passage lies not so much in this alleged application of a rather mistily dubious generalisation. More interesting is the direct proof which makes it clear that Burleigh is reading the first *Nihil* 'Nothing' of *Nihil est nihil* 'Nothing is nothing' as a syncategorematic expression, i.e. it is analogous to the 'No' of 'No *a* is *b*' rather than to a name which could figure as a substituend for the '*a*' in a form such as '*a* is *b*'. He had already distinguished these possibilities in an earlier analysis, wherein *nihil* 'nothing' was equated with *non-aliquid* 'not-something' in the style of the *quantificational* reading of Anselm's 'Nothing taught me to fly' example, mentioned above. Burleigh then further equated *this non-aliquid* 'not-something' with *quilibet non* ... 'anyone you please ... not ...' which was the contextually required correlate of the *quodlibet non* 'Anything you please ... not ...' of the present passage (*BDP* 224.14.24). (The other possibility, namely that of construing 'nothing' categorematically throughout the sentence 'Nothing is nothing', i.e. as though 'nothing' were a substituend in an '*a* is *b*' form, is what Anselm appears to be exploiting at one point (*HL* §6.64). However, under these circumstances the '. . . is . . .' must here be taken to be elliptical in such a fashion that a sentence such as 'Only all nothing is nothing', i.e.

.17 $\wedge \circ \wedge$

would be a full expression thereof; otherwise it would not be true (cf. II §5.31 and *HL* §6.641.5). Clearly, were that '. . . is . . .' to be identified with the primitive '. . . $\in$ . . .' of Ontology, then in view of .7 the resulting sentence is no longer true.)

A direct analysis of Burleigh's remarks shows that the equivalences he claims to reveal are in fact correct and embody theses of Ontology. Thus *Quodlibet est aliquid* 'Anything you please is something' becomes

.18 $[a]: a \in a . \supset . a \in \vee$ (cf. .2)

This has the form of a weak inclusion (II §4.3.5): 'Every thing is something' would be an alternative expression. Again, *Quodlibet non nihil est* 'Anything you please is not nothing' becomes:

.19 $[a]: a \in a . \supset . \sim (a \in \wedge)$ (cf. .7)

This in its turn has the form of a weak exclusion (II §4.3.8) and could be read as 'No thing is nothing', which yields immediately the pre-supposed sense of 'Nothing is nothing' with which Burleigh equates it. Finally .19 may be equated with the negation of its corresponding partial inclusion (II §4.3.6), namely:

.20 $\sim ([\exists a] . a \in a . a \in \wedge)$ (cf. .19)

i.e. it is *not* the case that *some thing* is nothing. Here we have the move corresponding to Burleigh's own from *quodlibet non . . .* 'Anything you please . . . not . . .' to *non-aliquid* 'not-something' described above.

Expressions .18, .19, and .20, as well as Burleigh's sentences which correspond to them, show how simple quantificational considerations of the sort which can be made to cluster round the traditional 'square of opposition', and which are probably a basis of Burleigh's intuitions here, can cooperate with the nominal use of 'nothing' for the purpose of analysing the sophisma in question. In a system employing re-stricted quantification analyses exemplifying such a high degree of sympathetic illumination of Burleigh's material would be totally impossible.

§5   OCKHAM AND THE FORMAL DISTINCTION

Thus far our attention has been confined to problems which would generally be described as logical ones. Now we turn to the first of four essays in the interpretation of matters more metaphysical. There is plainly no reason why Leśniewski's Ontology should not be of service here, since it constitutes, along with other Leśniewskian systems, a *corpus* which could aptly be referred to as a form of deductive metaphysics.

It is scarcely an exaggeration to assert that if one wished to select a single cardinal point on which the whole history of western thought turned, then the Scotist *distinctio formalis a parte rei* 'formal distinction on the side of the thing' would be a most prominent candidate for selection. Ockhamism is, to a large extent, a reaction against it, and in the absence of such a reaction the total complexion and subsequent history of European philosophy, logic, and theology would have been quite other than it in fact has been. In order to make intelligible some of the issues involved, I propose to examine Ockham's rejection of the distinction, a rejection which has the virtues of clarity and conciseness in the version given of it in pt I, ch. 16 of his *Summa Logicae*. A preliminary semiformal account of the controversy was presented in I §3, and is correlated by cross-references with the present section.

From the text mentioned we may gather that Ockham's central problem (and indeed *our* problem) is to make sense of the Scotist preparedness to assert:

(i) that there is a 'formal' distinction, in respect of an individual thing, between the common nature in question (i.e. a universal) and the individual 'difference'. For example, in the case of the individual human being named 'Socrates' such a distinction holds between his human nature and the ultimate individuating property (i.e. *Sorteitas* 'Socraticity') which makes Socrates into *this* human being. More generally, in the absence of some proper name, such an ultimate individuating difference is the *haecceitas* 'thisness' of the individual.

(ii) that this distinction is *a parte rei* (i.e. is a truth about how things are, and is not just conceptual, a mere 'distinction of reason').

(iii) that although from (i) and (ii) it does follow that universals are outside the mind, they must not be taken to be additional entities over and above and distinct from individuals.

In order to solve the problem proposed, recourse may once again be had to the Ontology described in Part II. Since the definitions within this system all stem from a single and simply comprehended primitive term, the degree of intelligibility which is thus made available is of the very highest order, and may serve to dispel some of the puzzles which, from the time of its first being enunciated, have clustered around the distinction in question. Since this section is only concerned with the elucidation of Scotist and Ockhamist theses by means of their

translations into sentences involving semantical categories which are
made available by definitions framed in the language of Ontology,
no Ontological theses other than definitional ones need be referred
to. From II §4.3.10 we already know that one may define singular
identity ('... = ...') thus:

.1 $[ab] : a = b . \equiv . a \in b . b \in a$

This definition is plainly such as to demand that for the proposition
of the form '$a = b$' to be true, the arguments of the '$=$' should be
unshared noun expressions. However, since the name-variables which
occur in Ontology may also take shared and fictitious names as
substituends, a further form of identity which is not restricted to
unshared names in order to express a truth is definable thus:

.2 $[ab] :. a \circ b . \equiv : [c] : c \in a . \equiv . c \in b$ (cf. II §4.3.12)

The functor of nominal conjunction ('... $\cap$ ...') which forms a
compound nominal expression from two nominal expressions, and
which was first encountered in §1.7, may again be noted:

.3 $[abc] : a \in b \cap c . \equiv . a \in b . a \in c$

Next, with the help of weak identity (.2) we may recall the definition
of an 'is' ('$\in$') of higher type which, unlike the primitive 'is' ('ϵ') of
Ontology, takes verbs or verb-like expressions (as opposed to names)
as arguments (cf. II §5.19):

.4 $[\varphi\psi] :: \varphi \in \psi . \equiv :. [\exists a] . \varphi(a) . \psi(a) :. [bc] : \varphi(b) .$
           $\varphi(c) . \supset . b \circ c$

Here 'φ' and 'ψ' are variables taking as substituends verbs (predicates)
or verb-like expressions. 'To run is to move' contains an 'is' which
could be analysed as shown in .4. Given .4, then all the functors
definable in terms of the primitive, lower-order 'is' ('ϵ') have, as
pointed out in II §5, their correlates in terms of this higher-order 'is'.
For example, one may characterise a higher-order singular identity,
the analogue of the lower-order singular identity (.1) thus:

.5 $[\varphi\psi] : \varphi = \psi . \equiv . \varphi \in \psi . \psi \in \varphi$ (cf. II §5.20)

In the present work we have been able hitherto to assume that the
diversity of argument signs (e.g. 'a' and 'b' in .1, 'φ' and 'ψ' in .5) will
suffice to show forth the diversity of semantical category which holds
between the '$=$' of .1 and the '$=$' of .5. As, however, there will occur
below occasions on which category-mistakes in respect of singular
identities have to be analysed, it is essential that the two types of
identity should be discriminable independently of their argument-
signs. In the present section, therefore, the lower-order singular

identity (.1) will henceforward have its argument-places bracketed thus:

.6   (   ) = (   )

and the higher-order singular identity (.5) will have its argument-places bracketed thus:

.7   {   } = {   }

This convention for brackets corresponds to the one proposed in the preliminary survey, I §3, .3 and .4.

The manner in which quantification was explained in II §2 has the result that quantification over predicate variables such as that which occurs in .4 and .5 does not commit one to the existence of 'abstract entities'. From II §5 we have the possibility of defining certain verbs or verb-like expressions (i.e. values of 'φ', 'ψ', etc.) which are formed from names, as in the following case:

.8 $[ab] : \mathrm{Cl}[\![a]\!](b) . \equiv . b \circ a$ (cf. II §5.18)

Here '$\mathrm{Cl}[\![\ ]\!]$', the functor defined, may be read off as 'form(ing) the class of . . .', or as 'to be a . . .', and so on, according to the context of its occurrence. This verb, in conjunction with the higher-order '$\in$' (.4) is used in the hitherto unmentioned definition which now follows:

.9 $[a\varphi] : a \in \mathrm{el}[\![\varphi]\!] . \equiv . [\exists b] . \varphi \in \mathrm{Cl}[\![b]\!] . a \in b$

The *definiendum* 'el$[\![\ ]\!]$' could here be read as 'element of the class determined by . . .', but will be used as an interpretation of the 'in being' of a 'nature' in a, so that a substituend for 'φ' for this purpose would be the 'name' of a common *natura* or *essentia*; that such essence-names are akin to verbs accords with the suggestions of *LAS*. This latter is, in its turn, in striking agreement with Aquinas' position as stated in his *In Boetii De Hebdomadibus*, lec. 2, n. 21 (cf. §6). Finally, a higher-level 'and', analogous to the one defined by .3, may be characterised by:

.10 $[\varphi\psi\chi] : \varphi \in \psi \cap \chi . \equiv . \varphi \in \psi . \psi \in \varphi$

We turn now to pt I, ch. 16 of Ockham's *Summa Logicae* wherein he gives a statement and criticism of the *distinctio formalis a parte rei* 'thing-centric formal distinction' (hereinafter referred to as the 'formal distinction'). It will be both convenient and reasonable to accept his statement as a fair one, as he could scarcely be in a better position for the formulation of such a statement. Although, he says, it is obvious to many that the universal is not some substance existing outside the mind and in individuals, while remaining really distinct from them, it still appears to some people (i.e. the Scotists) that the universal is in some fashion outside the mind and in individuals, but not in reality distinct from those individuals. (For some preliminary remarks about universals, see I §3.) He then goes on to exemplify this general thesis in terms of a concrete example; thus in respect of the human being Socrates the Scotists would assert the following:

S1 Human nature is 'in' Socrates.

S2 Human nature is 'contracted' to Socrates by an appropriate 'individual difference'.

S3 The individual difference mentioned in S2 is *formally* distinct from the human nature mentioned in S1; (this is a case of the formal distinction).

S4 The individual difference mentioned in S2 and the human nature mentioned in S1 are not really distinct; i.e. are not two things (*non sunt duae res*).

('Human nature' is, of course, the example of the 'universal' mentioned above.)

These tenets may now be elucidated in terms of Ontology and the nominal constants used by Ockham in his examples. It is not claimed that this elucidation of the formal distinction is sufficient to account for *all* the applications which Scotus makes of it, but only that it clarifies his intentions in instances of the sort here exemplified. Let us use 's' as an abbreviation for the unshared name 'Socrates' and '**h**' as an abbreviation for the shared name *homo* 'man'. On the assumption that these two names are comparatively unproblematical, our next need is to introduce in an intelligible manner the abstract universal quasi-nominal expression *natura humana* 'human nature' (or *humanitas* 'humanity') abbreviated as 'α', which corresponds to the concrete term '**h**'; likewise we need the abstract term denoting the individual difference corresponding to the unshared name 's' (i.e. we need *Sorteitas* 'Socraticity', abbreviated as 'σ'). In fact both of these introductions may be effected by means of the following two exemplifications of a suitable frame (cf. §6.18):

.11 $[\varphi]::\varphi \in \boldsymbol{\alpha} . \equiv :. \varphi \in \varphi :. [a] : a \in \text{el}[\![\varphi]\!] . \equiv . a \in \mathbf{h}$
.12 $[\varphi]::\varphi \in \boldsymbol{\sigma} . \equiv :. \varphi \in \varphi :. [a] : a \in \text{el}[\![\varphi]\!] . \equiv . a \in \mathbf{s}$

In .11 'α' is derived from '**h**' by the use of the functors defined above; likewise 'σ' is derived from '**s**' in .12. S1 may now be expressed:

.13 $\mathbf{s} \in \text{el}[\![\boldsymbol{\alpha}]\!]$

An interpretation of S2 may be approached by considering that the following is true:

.14 $\mathbf{s} \in \text{el}[\![\boldsymbol{\sigma}]\!]$

i.e. Socraticity is in Socrates; alternatively, Socrates has Socraticity. Combining .13 and .14 we have:

.15 $s \in el[\![\alpha \cap \sigma]\!]$

i.e. Socrates has Socratic-humanity; this suffices for the expression of S2. The '$\cap$' of .15 is that 'defined' at .10.

That the individual difference (Socraticity) is formally distinct from human nature, as claimed by S3, is expressible by:

.16 $\sim (\{\sigma\} = \{\alpha\})$

(cf. I §3.11 for a preliminary semiformal version.)

Finally, the statement in S4 that the individual difference (i.e. σ) and human nature (i.e. α), notwithstanding the truth of .16, are not 'really distinct', i.e. are not two things (*duae res*) in the sense in which Plato and Socrates are two things, amounts to the realisation that the following expression embodies a category-mistake:

.17 $\sim ((\sigma) = (\alpha))$

Here, as the brackets enclosing the argument-names show forth, 'σ' and 'α' are being used as arguments of a functor which should take names as its arguments, whereas 'σ' and 'α' are verb-like in nature, as is plain from .11 and .12. Thus, while a negation such as

.18 $\sim ((a) = (b))$

does indeed ensure that a and b are not the same individual object, .17 is nonsense owing to the nature of the arguments of '$(\ ) = (\ )$'.

Before passing on to examine some of Ockham's criticisms, it may be observed that the Scotist tenets have now been given a comparatively unproblematical interpretation in terms of Ontology, an interpretation which gives a true 'formal distinction' (i.e. in accordance with the suggestions of I §3 and III §2, one which is at the level of a higher-order functor such as '$\{\ \} = \{\ \}$'). This distinction is indeed *a parte rei* 'thing-centric', since .16 is a truth about how things are; it is not about words or 'intentions' of the mind. At the same time it does not commit one to the existence of separate Platonic abstract formal objects called *Sorteitas* 'Socraticity' and *humanitas* 'humanity'. The most vexed question of Scotus-lore has been the problem as to how one could reconcile the apparently anti-Platonic claim that the universal is not an extra-mental substance distinct from individuals with the claim that the formal distinction (e.g. between Socrates' individuating difference and human nature) is *a parte rei* 'thing-centric'. Since the only way in which critics have been able to construe the second claim has been in a Platonic manner, Scotus has been credited with Platonic realism, notwithstanding the first claim.

The analysis now provided shows precisely how both claims may be maintained simultaneously without a commitment to Platonic realism.

Ockham's basic confusion in the criticisms which follow lies in his assumption that a negation such as .16 can really only be of the sort shown at .18: _numquam potest esse aliqua distinctio qualiscumque extra animam, nisi ubi res distinctae sunt_ 'there can never be any extra-mental distinction apart from the case in which distinct objects are involved'. This has as a consequence the following glaring sophism: he assumes that the denial of a real (i.e. lower-order) distinction in S4 amounts to the assertion of a real non-distinction (i.e. one involving a lower-order identity like .1) between the universal nature and the in-dividual difference: _universale et differentia individualis sunt eadem res_ 'the universal and the individuating difference are the same object'. In point of fact, as has been indicated, the denial contained in S4 surely expresses the realisation that an expression having the form of .17 embodies a category-mistake, i.e. S4 is _not_ the denial of a negation such as .18: it does _not_ have the form:

.19 $\quad \sim (\sim ((a) = (b)))$

which has as a consequence:

.20 $\quad (a) = (b)$

This latter is the consequence which Ockham is drawing in the quotation just cited. On the contrary, S4 needs to be taken as the rejection as nonsense of the whole pattern of expression shown in .17, embodying an obvious category-mistake. Accordingly, since the main weight of Ockham's objections is directed against the position of someone who maintains that a real (i.e. lower-order) identity like .20 holds between the nature and the individual difference, his attack tends to be totally beside the point. For example, his second and third objections claim that this allegedly real identity commits one to the absurdity of holding that the same object is both common (in respect of the universal nature) and proper (in respect of the individuating difference), i.e. opposite predications attributable to the same in-dividual ensue. True, given .13, .14, and .15, one might in a loose fashion of speaking say that the same object (e.g. Socrates) is in some sense constituted by both a universal (i.e. α) and an individual difference (i.e. σ); a charitable interpretation of these objections might lead one to assume that this 'constitution' is here the object of Ockham's attack. Nevertheless, the definitions which have been sug-gested above, especially .11 and .12, are such that the objections, when thus interpreted, can be reduced to the absurd claims that a common noun and a proper noun cannot refer to the same individual, and that these opposite qualifications ('common' and 'proper') applying as they do to two names referring to the same individual, apply also to that individual.

Again, Ockham's insensitivity to the possibility of a distinction of the sort shown in .16 holding extra-mentally without being of the sort shown in .18 leads him to insist that *any* extra-mental distinction which is a truth about how things are (e.g. .16) must involve one of the sort shown in .18: *si ergo inter istam naturam* [*scil. humanitas*] *et istam differentiam* [*scil. Sorteitas*] *sit qualiscumque distinctio, oportet quod sint res realiter distinctae* 'if therefore there is a distinction of any sort whatsoever between this nature [i.e. humanity] and this individual difference [i.e. Socraticity], then these two must be really distinct objects'. This amounts to asserting, for instance, that

.21 $\sim (\{\alpha\} = \{\sigma\}) \mathbin{.} \supset \mathbin{.} \sim ((\alpha) = (\sigma))$

This is, of course, sheer confusion; it has already been amply demonstrated that the consequent of .21 is nonsense owing to the inappropriateness of the arguments to the functor there used.

In the absence of an artificial language the variety of whose semantical categories rivals or exceeds that of those available in the language undergoing analysis, any discussion of medieval logical and philosophical problems runs the risk of being beside the point. Ordinary non-technical language lacks this variety, so that when an encounter such as that which has just been sketched occurs, one inevitably tends, in the absence of the requisite logical co-ordinates, to take the naïve Ockhamist view, or to suspect Scotus of Platonism. In point of fact a thorough examination will probably reveal that many of those accused by historians of logic of being Platonic realists are in fact gifted with a subtle sensitivity as to the semantical possibilities of language.

§6   BEING, ESSENCE AND EXISTENCE

In continuation of the more metaphysical strain initiated in the foregoing section, a tentative set of conjectures as to some threads of the sense of St Thomas Aquinas' discourse concerning *essentia* 'essence' and *esse* 'to-be' is now presented. The flexibility of Ontology is such that these conjectures are susceptible of any further qualification which may be required in order to bring them into line with the finer points of Aquinas' theory; in other words, there is nothing final about their every detail. Further, no attempt is made hereunder to reproduce features of Aquinas' thought apart from certain aspects of the topics in question. Thus the distinction of substance from accident, with its accompanying notion that an accident is *magis entis quam ens* 'an of-a-being rather than a being' have not been accounted for hereunder. Nor have the connections between essence and existence, on the one hand, and the notions of actuality and capacity on the other, been touched upon. Although the final result may therefore overlap Aquinas' thought in a comparatively meagre fashion, any apparent contact between his system and a modern one is surely worth exploring.

The Ontology of Part II is already a theory of *ens in quantum ens* 'being as such', and so carries into effect, using the resources of modern logic, the project originally conceived in Aristotle's *Metaphysica* (*LR* 150). It now becomes important to recall that quantification, as used in the present work, is unrestricted, thereby allowing the dissociation of somehood and existence, so that the latter may be accounted for in notation distinct from quantifier notation. Hence '∃ . . .' is read as 'For some . . .' and not as 'There exists an . . . such that . . .' (cf. II §2.25 and *LLE*). This makes Ontology particularly suitable for dealing with questions concerning *esse* 'to-be'.

The theses to be used in this section have already been encountered or used on previous occasions in the present work, but may be briefly represented for ease of reference. Thus we have:

.1 $[ab] :: a \in b . \equiv : . [\exists c] . c \in a : . [c] : c \in a . \supset . c \in b : .$
        $[cd] : c \in a . d \in a . \supset . c \in d$ (cf. II §5.1)

.2 $[a] : \mathrm{ob}(a) . \equiv . [\exists b] . a \in b$ (cf. II §2.233, §4.3.10)

.3 $[ab] : a = b . \equiv . a \in b . b \in a$ (cf. II §2.233, §4.3.3)

.4 $[ab] : . a \circ b . \equiv : [c] : c \in a . \equiv . c \in b$ (cf. II §2.223, §4.3.12)

.5 $[a\varphi] : a \in \mathrm{trm}\langle\varphi\rangle . \equiv . a \in a . \varphi(a)$ (cf. II §5.15)

.6 $[ab] : \mathrm{Cl}[\![b]\!](a) . \equiv . a \circ b$ (cf. II §5.18)

.7 $[\varphi\psi] :: \varphi \in \psi . \equiv : . [\exists a] . \varphi(a) . \psi(a) : . [bc] : \varphi(b) .$
        $\varphi(c) . \supset . b \circ c$ (cf. II §5.19)

.8 $[a\varphi] : a \in \mathrm{el}[\![\varphi]\!] . \equiv . [\exists b] . \varphi \in \mathrm{Cl}[\![b]\!] . a \in b$
                                  (cf. III §5.6, .7 and .9)

.9 $[a\varphi] : \mathrm{Cl}[\varphi](a) . \equiv . \mathrm{Cl}[\![\mathrm{trm}\langle\varphi\rangle]\!](a)$
                                  (cf. .5, .6 and II §5.21)

.10 $[a] : a \in \vee . \equiv . a \in a$ (cf. II §4.3.13, III §4.2)

A preliminary version of some of the points now to be made was presented in I §3, and may be consulted as a guide to the present material, should the need for elementary elucidation be felt.

The elucidation of Aquinas' uses of *essentia* 'essence' and *esse* 'to-be' may be undertaken by considering the fact that he would accept the following three sentences as truths:

.11   *albedo est quo album est album* 'whiteness is that by which a white is white'

.12   *humanitas est quo homo est homo* 'humanity is that by which
       a man is a man'
.13   *esse est quo substantia est ens* 'to-be is that by which a
       substance is a being'

(see, for instance, *ACG* II 54, *AST* I q. 3 a. 3). The important point
to note here is the parallelism which shows itself between .11 and .12,
on the one hand, and .13 on the other: the first two are concerned
with the 'essences' whiteness and humanity, but the third is about
esse 'to-be'. In view of this parallelism it may be conjectured that if
cases like .11 and .12 can be understood, then the key to the understanding of .13 will be available. Now in .11 and .12 *albedo* 'whiteness'
and *humanitas* 'humanity' are the essences which, as the two following
Aquinate commonplaces demonstrate, are possessed by whites and
men respectively:

.14   *album est habens albedinem* 'a white is a whiteness-haver'
.15   *homo est habens humanitatem* 'a man is a humanity-haver'

(cf. I §3(b)). Further, by generalising from .14 and .15, one can regard
the following as an Aquinate thesis:

.16   *omne ens est essentiam habens* 'every be-er is an essence-haver'
                                                         (cf. I §3.6)

(The application of .16 is restricted to *entia per participationem*, i.e.
beings which have ('participate in') their essences, and are hence
different from Aquinas' 'pure forms' (angels) which *are* their essences;
cf. I §3.) In its turn .16 reminds one of the following well-known adage
of St Thomas:

.17   *omne ens est esse habens* 'every being is a to-be haver'

(The application of .17 extends to all beings except God, who is
identical with his *esse* 'to-be'; cf. I §3.) We are now in a position such
that if an elucidation of .16 is possible, then a key to the interpretation
of .17, and hence to Aquinas' discourse concerning *esse* 'to-be' will
be within our reach, given also the parallelism already evident in
.11, .12, and .13 above.

The project outlined in the last paragraph imposes various tasks.
First we must attempt to situate abstract nouns (e.g. *albedo* 'whiteness',
humanitas 'humanity') within the terms made available by the language
of Ontology. Given definitions .7 and .8 above, it is possible to relate
such nouns to rather more unproblematic ones such as *albus* 'white'
and *homo* 'man' by means of the following frame:

.18 $[\varphi] :: \varphi \in \Psi \, . \equiv : . \, \varphi \in \varphi : . \, [a] : a \in \mathrm{el}[\![\varphi]\!] \, . \equiv . \, a \in \mathbf{X}$

(Exemplifications of this frame have been encountered at §5.11 and .12). By the use of .18, given, for instance, *albus* 'white' in the place of '**X**', one can assign a sense to *albedo* 'whiteness', which would then stand correspondingly in the place of '**Ψ**'. This treatment of abstract nouns presupposes that they are in fact more akin to verbs (i.e. values of 'φ', 'ψ'. etc.) than to nouns, and is due to C. Lejewski (cf. *LAS*). At the same time it is in entire accord with Aquinas' doctrine in his *In Boetii De Hebdomadibus* lec. 2, n. 21, wherein *currere* 'to run' (a possible argument, verb-like in nature, of the higher-order '$\in$' which figures in the left-hand proposition of .18) is said to signify abstractly, as does *albedo* 'whiteness', and both are contrasted with *currens* 'runner' and *album* 'white' respectively (i.e. possible arguments, nominal in nature, of the lower-order, primitive '$\in$' of Ontology which figures in the extreme right-hand proposition of .18). In view of these facts it is apparent that 'el$[\![\mathbf{\Psi}]\!]$' (cf. .8), wherein the sense of '**Ψ**' has been related to that of '**X**' as shown in .18, suffices to represent Aquinas' sense of *habens* **X**-*eitas* '**X**-ness haver' (where **X**-*eitas* '**X**-ness' is the abstract noun corresponding to '**X**'). Now such abstract nouns in some way signify essences; in fact *essentia* 'essence' is a quasi-common-name which 'refers' to *albedo* 'whiteness', *humanitas* 'humanity', and the like. In relation to functors already defined (.6, .7) *essentia* 'essence' may be understood as 'Cl' as it occurs in the following:

.19 $\quad [\varphi] : \varphi \in \text{Cl} \,.\equiv.\, [\exists a]\,.\, \varphi \in \text{Cl}[\![a]\!]$

Thus, given that one of the various ways in which *ens* 'being' (as a name, not a participle) may be rendered is by means of 'v' (defined .10), the thesis *omne ens est essentiam habens* 'every being is an essence-haver' (.16 above), along with its obviously true converse, amounts to:

.20 $\quad [a] : a \in \text{v} \,.\equiv.\, [\exists\varphi]\,.\, a \in \text{el}[\![\varphi]\!]\,.\, \varphi \in \text{Cl}$ (cf. I §3.6)

(i.e. for all *a*, *a* is a being if and only if for some φ, *a* is a haver of φ-ness, and φ is an essence). On the assumption that the 'φ' of 'el$[\![\varphi]\!]$' has been built up on the lines indicated in .18, and recollecting that 'el$[\![\varphi]\!]$' thus represents *habens . . . eitas* 'having . . . ness', we see that .20 not only ensures that the values of 'φ' are *essentia* 'essences', but also shows forth the correlation between *having an essence* and *being a being*, i.e. a totally unproblematic elucidation of the Aquinate position as regards the essential aspect of *entia per participationem* (beings characterisable by 'having . . . ness') other than pure forms is now available. True, in the absence of further restrictions on the nature of the non-abstract nouns which can stand in the place of '**X**' in .18, the expression .20 has a wider sense than Aquinas would wish

it to have. Thus, were proper nouns (e.g. 'Socrates', 'this') eligible
to take the place of the '**X**' mentioned, then Scotist individuating
essences (*Sorteitas* 'Socraticity', *haecceitas* 'thisness') would be com-
prised in the generalisation which .20 represents (cf. I §3, III §5). An
appropriate restriction in respect of .18 must therefore be imposed
if .20 is to be understood in a strictly Aquinate sense.

The sense of .16 having thus been resolved, it now remains to
discover a verb which will serve as a value of 'φ' in .20, but which
will convey the fact that it is the having of *esse* 'to-be', rather than
of an *essentia* 'essence', which is in question, and thus elucidate .4.
One of Aquinas' own remarks gives an exact indication as to the
verb needed: *esse cuiuslibet rei consistit in indivisione . . . unumquodque
sicut custodit suum esse, ita custodit suam unitatem* 'The to-be of any
thing is constituted by its being exactly one . . . each and every thing
keeps its to-be to the extent that it keeps its oneness' (*AST* I q. 11
a. 1, c). (The first part of this statement sounds like a deliberately-
amended version of Anselm of Canterbury's *esse uniuscuiusque rei in
definitione consistat* 'the being of each and every thing is constituted
by its definition' (*HDG* 3.800) which itself is a derivation from
similarly worded statements in Boethius (*B* 1196C)). Clearly, at this
point Aquinas has in mind a truth such as that conveyed by the following thesis of Ontology:

.21 $[ab] : . \ \mathrm{ob}(a) . \supset : [cd] . c \in a . d \in a . \supset . c = d$

This thesis follows from the axiom of Ontology (.1) and definitions
.2 and .3 above; it indicates the connection between exactly-one-hood
and 'indivision' which is in question here. It suggests also that 'ob( )'
(i.e. 'There exists exactly one . . .') is the verb required for our declared
purpose of finding a value of 'φ' in .20 suitable for the elucidation
of .17.

In order, however, to fit the verb 'ob( )' to become an argument
of 'el$[\![\ \ ]\!]$' as defined at .8, we need first of all to compound from it
a nominal form which can stand as a value of 'b' in .8. This is quite
easily done by the use of 'trm$\langle\varphi\rangle$' (defined .5), so as the appropriate
instance of .8 we have:

.22 $[a] : a \in \mathrm{el}[\![\mathrm{Cl}[\![\mathrm{trm}\langle\mathrm{ob}\rangle]\!]]\!] . \equiv . \mathrm{Cl}[\![\mathrm{trm}\langle\mathrm{ob}\rangle]\!] \in \mathrm{Cl}[\![\mathrm{trm}\langle\mathrm{ob}\rangle]\!] .$
          $a \in \mathrm{trm}\langle\mathrm{ob}\rangle$

Further, in view of definition .9, 'Cl$[\![\mathrm{trm}\langle\mathrm{ob}\rangle]\!]$' may be contracted to
'Cl$[\mathrm{ob}]$', so that the left-hand side of .22, which is going to figure
in the *esse* 'to be' parallel of .20, will read '$a \in \mathrm{el}[\![\mathrm{Cl}[\mathrm{ob}]]\!]$'. Hence,
using 'Cl$[\mathrm{ob}]$' as a value of 'φ' in .20, we have the analogous thesis:

.23 $[a] : a \in \mathrm{v} . \equiv . a \in \mathrm{el}[\![\mathrm{Cl}[\mathrm{ob}]]\!] . \mathrm{Cl}[\mathrm{ob}] \in \mathrm{Cl}$

The second conjunct on the right-hand side of this expression shows a sense in which one could, if one wished, speak of the essence of *esse* 'to-be'. This would, strictly speaking, not be one of Aquinas' points, and as that second conjunct is in any case a thesis it may be dropped. The required expression of .17, i.e. of *omne ens est esse habens* 'every being is a to-be haver' (along with its obviously true converse) thus becomes:

.24 $[a] : a \in v . \equiv . a \in \text{el} [\![\text{Cl} [\text{ob}]]\!]$ (cf. I §3.7)

(i.e. for all *a*, *a* is a being if and only if *a* is a haver of exactly-one-ness). Once again, this result accords exactly with Aquinas' remarks in *In Boetii De Hebdomadibus*, wherein *esse* 'to-be', *currere* 'to run', and *albedo* 'whiteness' (all verb-like) are contrasted with *ens* 'being', *currens* 'runner', and *album* 'white' respectively (all nominal). In .24 'Cl[ob]' is the verb which corresponds with '*esse*', and 'v' is the noun corresponding to *ens* 'being'.

Now it is perfectly evident that both the key Aquinate theses here undergoing investigation, i.e. .16 and .17, have senses which are capable of indefinitely large analogous extension. As far as we have gone in our analyses above, both .20 and .24, their respective interpretations, remain pitched at only the level of the primitive lower-order '∈', with a correspondingly lower-order sense of 'v' (*ens* 'being'), whereas the possibility of indefinitely many ascending orders of '∈' (as initiated in definition .17) yields also the possibility of indefinitely many corresponding orders of sense of 'v' (*ens* 'being'). Hence if it is granted that the present section has at least illuminated some small portion of what amounts to a segment of the lower-order sense of Aquinas' maxims, one can begin to glimpse more concretely their tremendous complexity when interpreted analogously. Use of the relevant definitions of the functors involved in .20 and .24 for the spelling out of their lower-order senses alone will convey in a concrete fashion the nature of only one dimension of this complexity. Little wonder, therefore, that (as suggested in §1, §2) talk at the 'formal' level was eagerly grasped as a tool for maintaining this sort of discourse in the absence of a totally artificial language. Again, it is little wonder that controversies over its handling should arise, as seen in §5. In the face of these complexities it is all too tempting to abandon, with Ockham, the attempt to bring them under control, and to try to do all that is required at the level of the lower-order, name-flanked 'is'.

Our excursion into analysis suggest that it is perfectly possible to sympathise with all parties in such controversies. On the one hand, justice is done to those who wish to take seriously discourse at the 'formal' level (e.g. Thomists and Scotists). On the other hand, the

Ockhamist aim of taking the obscurity out of such discourse is accomplished by showing how it may be based on the primitive name-flanked 'ε' of Ontology. Unfortunately, as §5 suggests, Ockham seems to have imagined that the various levels of discourse (e.g. concerning distinctions) were somehow exclusive: one could not, he appears to hold, accept them all. That this is not so should be now be evident.

It would appear that such suppositions of exclusiveness, arising from an insufficient appreciation of the possibility of a deductively mediating background (such as has been attempted in the present work) may be responsible for many of the controversies (and hence developments) in the relevant segments of medieval thought. Such segments, although the fruit of various schools, constitute a rich and unmapped continent of truths of deductive metaphysics for the unified exploration of which some rudimentary instruments and methods are being herein proffered.

§7   THE ONTOLOGICAL ARGUMENT

The proofs which occur in the second and third chapters of St Anselm's *Proslogion* have exercised the minds of philosophers almost from the first moment of their publication. Are the proofs valid? Are the proofs intended as rational enterprises which stand independently of the faith of their propounder or do they only have validity (whatever this may mean) within the ambit of a pre-existing faith? If the proofs are invalid, what exactly is their defect? On all these counts there still subsists disagreement which has only been augmented by the recent revival of serious interest in the proofs.

The ultimate purpose of the present section, and the one which is directly connected with the main theme of the present work, is merely to go as far as possible with Anselm, given the simple means already at our disposal, and to produce and examine forms of expression which at some points approximate to his own. In order to accomplish even this modest and limited purpose, however, a great deal of clearing of the ground is necessary. For instance, we must answer the question: what was the original point, in Anselm's mind, of the two chapters now undergoing scrutiny? This involves a certain amount of literary and historical investigation of a sort not found in previous sections of this present Part.

Justification of the obtrusion of this sort of investigation lies in the almost universally customary approach to the content of the two chapters mentioned, the text of which now follows. That approach is to be questioned. The accompanying translation has hence been kept as literal as possible, especially at the opening of ch. 3, as otherwise the full flavour and point of the original tends to disappear. This has led to some awkwardness of expression, unavoidable in the circumstances:

Proslogion, ch. 2

	That God truly is	*Quod vere sit deus*
1.0	Therefore, o Lord, who gives understanding to faith, as far as you know it to be profitable, grant that I may understand that	*Ergo, domine, qui das fidei intellectum, da mihi, ut quantum scis expedire intelligam, quia*
1.1	you are, as we believe [cf. 3.4] and	*es sicut credimus, et*
1.2	you are what we believe you are [cf. 4.50]	*hoc es quod credimus.*
2.0	And indeed, we believe that you are something than which nothing greater can be thought.	*Et quidem credimus te esse aliquid quo nihil maius cogitari possit.*
3.0	Or is there no such nature, since the fool has said in his heart 'There is no God'?	*An ergo non est aliqua talis natura, quia 'dixit insipiens in corde suo: non est deus'* [Ps. 13 et 52 (Vulg.)]?
3.10	But it is at least certain that that very fool, when he hears that which I am now saying, namely, 'something than which nothing greater can be thought' [cf. 2.0], understands that which he hears:	*Sed certe ipse idem insipiens, cum audit hoc ipsum quod dico: 'aliquid quo maius nihil cogitari potest', intelligit quod audit;*
3.110	and that which he understands is in his understanding,	*et quod intelligit in intellectu eius est,*
3.111	even though he does not understand it to exist.	*etiam si non intelligat illud esse.*
3.120	Now there is a difference between a thing's being in	*Aliud enim est rem esse in intellectu, aliud intelligere*

the understanding and its
being understood to exist.

rem esse.

3.121   For when the painter thinks
ahead to that which is to be
effected, he indeed has it in
his understanding, but does
not yet understand to exist
that which he has not yet
made.

*Nam cum pictor praecogitat
quae facturus est, habet
quidem in intellectu, sed
nondum intelligit quod
nondum fecit.*

3.122   When, however, he has
made the painting, he both
has it in his understanding
and understands to exist
that which he has now
effected.

*Cum vero iam pinxit, et
habet in intellectu et intelligit
esse quod iam fecit.*

3.130   Even the fool, therefore, is
committed to admitting that
there at least exists in the
understanding something
than which nothing greater
can be thought, for

*Convincitur ergo etiam
insipiens esse vel in intellectu
aliquid quo nihil maius
cogitari potest, quia*

3.131   when he hears of this, he
understands, and

hoc cum audit intelligit, et

3.132   whatsoever is understood is
in the understanding.

*quidquid intelligitur in
intellectu est.*

3.20   Further, it is certain that
that than which a more
great cannot be thought is
not able to be in the
understanding only,

*Et certe id quo maius cogitari
nequit, non potest esse in solo
intellectu.*

3.21   for if it is at least in the
understanding only, it can
be thought also to exist in
fact, and this is more great.

*Si enim vel in solo intellectu
est, potest cogitari esse et in
re, quod maius est.*

3.22   On this account, if that than
which a more great is not
able to be thought is in the
understanding only, then

*Si ergo id quo maius cogitari
non potest est in solo
intellectu,*

3.221	that very thing than which a more great is *not* able to be thought is that than which a more great *is* able to be thought.	*id ipsum quo maius cogitari non potest, est quo maius cogitari potest.*
3.3	But obviously this [3.221] cannot be.	*Sed certe hoc esse non potest.*
3.4	Hence without any doubt something than which a more great is not able to be thought exists both in the understanding and in fact [cf. 1.1].	*Existit ergo procul dubio aliquid quo maius cogitari non valet, et in intellectu et in re.*

Proslogion, ch. 3

	That he cannot be thought not to be	*Quod non possit cogitari non esse*
4.1	Which indeed is so truly that it is *not even possible* for it **to be thought** *not to be*.	*Quod utique sic vere est ut* nec **cogitari** possit non esse.
4.2	For something is *possible* **to be thought** *to be* which is *not possible* **to be thought** *not to be*,	*Nam* potest **cogitari** esse *aliquid quod* non potest **cogitari** non esse;
4.21	and this latter is greater than that which is *possible* **to be thought** *not to be*.	*quod maius est quam quod* non esse **cogitari** potest.
4.30	Whence if that than which a greater is not able to be thought is *possible* **to be thought** *not to be*, then	*Quare si id quo maius nequit cogitari* potest **cogitari** non esse,
4.31	that very thing than which a greater is not able to be thought is *not* that than which a greater is not able to be thought;	*id ipsum quo maius cogitari nequit non est id quo maius cogitari nequit:*
4.311	but this cannot be consistent.	*quod convenire non potest.*

4.4	So truly, therefore, is the something than which a greater is not able to be thought that it is not even able to be thought not to be.	*Sic ergo vere est aliquid quo maius cogitari non potest, ut nec cogitari possit non esse.*
4.50	And this is what you are, o Lord our God [cf. 1.2].	*Et hoc es tu, domine deus noster.*
4.51	So truly, therefore, are you, o Lord my God, that you are not even capable of being thought not to be.	*Sic ergo vere es, domine deus meus, ut nec cogitari possis non esse.*
4.511	And properly so, for if some mind were able to think something better than you, then would the creature rise above the creator, and would judge of the creator, and this is the height of absurdity. And indeed, whatsoever else is, apart from you alone, is capable of being thought not to be, since whatsoever else is is not so truly, and therefore has less being.	*Et merito. Si enim aliqua mens posset cogitare aliquid melius te, ascenderet creatura super creatorem, et iudicaret de creatore: quod valde est absurdum. Et quidem quidquid est aliud praeter te solum, potest cogitari non esse, quia quidquid aliud est non sic vere, et idcirco minus habet esse.*
4.512	Why, therefore, has the fool said in his heart 'God is not', when it is so obvious to the reasonable mind that you have being in the highest degree? Why, save because he is dull and a fool?	*Cur itaque dixit insipiens in corde suo, 'Non est deus', cum tam in promptu sit rationali menti te maxime omnium esse? Cur, nisi quia stultus et insipiens?* (*S* 101–3)

As we see, the respective headings of chs 2 and 3 are: *Quod vere sit deus* 'That God truly is', and *Quod non possit cogitari non esse* 'That he cannot be thought not to be'. They would therefore appear to be concerned with diverse questions. Yet it has become customary for ch. 3 to be taken to constitute part of, or an alternative version of, that proof of the existence of God which is the overtly stated aim of ch. 2. I am of the opinion that this customary approach is mistaken, and that the distinction of purpose implied by the headings is, in fact, to be taken seriously. Hence I must establish that the point of ch. 3 is indeed distinct from that of ch. 2. This will be effected by reference to evidence both extrinsic and intrinsic in relation to the content of those chapters. Having established this distinction, we may then go on to attempt to reproduce some of the effects contained in ch. 2.

Gaunilo, monk of Marmoutiers, was the first to object to Anselm's arguments. These objections are contained in his *Pro insipiente* 'On behalf of the fool'. Anselm in his turn composed a lengthy reply to these objections. We may now note, in the first place, that Anselm's own description of the nature of the contents of chs 2 and 4, Gaunilo's reactions to them, and the general structure of Anselm's reply to Gaunilo, all point to a pervading agreement as to the diverse purposes of those chapters. Thus Anselm's prayer in the first sentence of ch. 2 contains a twofold petition: that God's existence (*quia es sicut credimus* 'that you are, as we believe' (1.1)) and God's nature (*hoc es quod credimus* 'you are what we believe you are' (1.2)) should as far as possible be made plain to him. Now ch. 2 contains the proof of God's existence, and hence corresponds to the first petition, while ch. 3 initiates that description of the nature of God which was the object of the second petition, as the recurrence of the very words of that petition within this chapter confirm: *et hoc es tu, domine deus noster* 'and this is what you are, o Lord our God' (4.50). The respective chapter headings, although slightly later additions, likewise confirm this division.

Gaunilo's *Pro insipiente* 'On behalf of the fool' is again structured in a fashion which reflects the differing functions of the two chapters. Only after six chapters directed against Anselm's proof of the existence of God, as given in *Proslogion* 2, does Guanilo come, in his ch. 7, to deal with the material of *Proslogion* 3. That this material is seen by Gaunilo as covering a further issue, namely the nature rather than the existence of God, is implied by the *interim* 'for the present', *deinceps* 'in the next place' and *tale* 'of such a sort' of the opening words of this final stage of his objections: *Haec interim ad obiecta insipiens ille responderit* 'The fool can for the present make these replies to the objections raised' (i.e. thus far ch. 2 has been under discussion) . . . *cum deinceps asseritur tale esse maius illud, ut nec sola cogitatione valeat non esse* . . . '. . . when in the next place this greatest being is said to be of such a sort that not even for thought alone can it not be . . .' (i.e. the further point as to the nature of this greatest being is now to be broached). The *tale . . . ut nec . . .* 'of such a sort . . . that not even . . .' construction of this last sentence is a variant of that of Anselm's first sentence in *Proslogion* 3: *sic vere est, ut nec cogitari possit non esse* 'so truly is it that it cannot even be thought not to be'. The structure thus common to the two last-quoted sentences conveys the impression that for both Anselm and Gaunilo the impossibility of being thought not to exist is somehow a *consequence* of the existence of God which Anselm claims to have proved in *Proslogion* 2. This impression is confirmed by Gaunilo's double enlargement on such a consequence. First he says that the Fool of the psalms can question the fact of the existence of a greatest being of such a sort that thence as a consequence can be proved (*ut ex hoc mihi debeat probari*) its nature as a being whose non-existence is unthinkable. Secondly, and in a more general vein, he points out that a valid proof of the existence of God is required so that one may then proceed to deduce all the *other* properties which necessarily flow from God's nature: *ut ex hoc alia iam possumus omnia comprobare, quibus necesse est illud quod maius ac melius omnibus non carere*. In other words, Gaunilo regards Anselm as holding that 'being not thinkable as non-existent' is one property among many other properties, and the attribution of this property to God is in some way dependent upon God's having first been shown to exist. The way in which Anselm may view this dependence will be examined below.

Finally, Anselm's *Reply* to Gaunilo persists in this underlining of the diverse functions of *Proslogion* 2 and 3. The *Reply* falls into three main portions: chs 1 to 3 concern the *existence* of God (i.e. relate ultimately to the question of *Proslogion* 2), while ch. 4 has nothing at all to say on this question, but is solely concerned with replying to Gaunilo's ch. 7, examined in the last paragraph above; this ch. 4, therefore, relates ultimately to the material of *Proslogion* 3. The third and final phase of the *Reply*, i.e. chs 5 to 10, is clearly in the nature of an addition. As Anselm himself states at the beginning of ch. 5, he *had* intended to stop at this point, and not bother pursuing the refutation of further details. As, however, some readers are not satisfied with his reply as it stands, he will pursue such further refutation. From this it is evident that chs 1 to 4 of the *Reply* are an original draft, closely following the two-phase structure observable throughout the controversy, and that the presence of a third phase in the *Reply* hence does not affect that persistent dual structure. Anselm's own summary of results in ch. 10 of the *Reply* likewise distinguishes between the question of God's existence and that of God's nature: *probetur existere, et id ipsum esse quidquid de divina substantia oportet credere* 'he is proved to exist and to be whatsoever it is proper that the divine substance should be believed to be'.

The utter consistency of the division between the questions of chs 2 and 3 respectively of *Proslogion* throughout the controversy hence yields a strong indication that ch. 3 was envisaged by neither Anselm nor Gaunilo as an attempt to prove the existence of God. In other words, neither of the protagonists took it for granted that the proof that God cannot be thought not to exist entails the existence of God as a consequence. Indeed, it will be suggested below that it is rather the *converse* of such a consequence which emerges from the text of *Proslogion* 3.

Thus far our examination has been restricted to considerations extrinsic to the details of the content of ch. 3. According to its heading, it may be recalled, the aim of the chapter is to prove that God, whose existence has been proved in ch. 2, cannot be thought not to exist. The chapter's first paragraph begins by stating the entailment already noted above (*sic vere est ut nec cogitari possit non esse* 'so truly is he that he cannot even be thought not to be'), and only then is a proof of the chapter's thesis offered. The pattern of this proof follows that of ch. 2 in the sense that here, as in ch. 2, a *reductio ad absurdum* argument is offered. The assumption giving rise to the absurdity in ch. 3, however, is the supposition that God can be thought not to exist. I have already shown elsewhere (*HL* §5.5) that this chapter is closely connected with Anselm's modal logic as a whole. It will therefore suffice for the moment to summarise the following points. First, the modal expressions *posse non esse* 'to be possible not to be', *posse esse* 'to be possible to be', and *non posse non esse* 'to be not possible not to be', whose interrelations were the object of special study by Boethius and Anselm, all occur in the first paragraph of ch. 3 (4.1–4.30), but with *cogitari* 'to-be-thought' interposed; e.g. it is said that that of which *non potest cogitari non esse* 'it is not possible to be thought not to be' is true is greater than that of which *potest cogitari non esse* 'it is possible for it to be thought not to be' is true. Now such interpositions would be quite superfluous if, as is sometimes thought, the point of the chapter were to prove that God is a necessary being (and therefore exists). For when *cogitari* 'to-be-thought' is everywhere omitted (except, of course, within the expression used to describe God: *id quo maius cogitari nequit* 'that than which a greater cannot be thought' and its variants) the remainder of the text constitutes a proof that God is 'not possible not to be', i.e. is necessary. It looks, therefore, as though something more than a proof that God is a necessary being is here intended, the insertion of *cogitari* 'to-be-thought' into the modal expressions being a symptom of this further aim. What, then, is the precise import of this insertion? (The text of this passage, which is presented on p. 104, underlines these points by (i) italicising the stock modal expressions, and (ii) showing the interposed *cogitari* 'to-be-thought' in heavy type. This facilitates the experiment in re-reading which has just been proposed.)

The salient point, and one which is totally overlooked by most moderns, is that beings which are necessary (i.e. not possible not to be) are, according to the Boethian cosmological background of the commentaries from which Anselm draws his modal logic, comparatively commonplace. One has only to look up into the night sky to see evidence of many such beings. The heavenly bodies provide Boethius with a set of standard examples of necessary beings. Hence to prove that God was a necessary being, or that God necessarily existed, would scarcely be a way of exalting God above his creation. Remarks made by Boethius and Gerbert (cf. *HLA* §5.54) suggest that one reason why *cogitari* 'to-be-thought' is inserted, so that *non potest* cogitari *non esse* 'he is not possible *to be thought* not to be' becomes true of God, was to exalt the being of God above that of the many created necessary beings which are such that thought *can* decompose them. Hence while these other necessary beings are not possible not to be, they can nevertheless be *thought* not to be. The divine simplicity, in contrast, and as is argued in chs 18 and 22 of *Proslogion*, is unique in resisting the decomposing power of thought. It is this sort of exaltation, rather than any further proof of the existence of God based in his being a mere necessary being, which is part of the true point of this ch. 3. The distinction between essence and existence, together with the stress on divine aseity, performs an analogous function in the work of Aquinas.

Further, it might with some feasibility be conjectured that for Anselm God was *not*, strictly speaking, a necessary being. Anselm's dominant interpretation of necessity as involving constraint or prevention suggests this. As he says in *Cur Deus Homo* II, 17, *Omnis ... necessitas est aut coactio aut prohibitio* 'All necessity is a form of either coercion or prohibition'. He expressly uses this interpretation to deprecate the attribution of necessity to God: *Cum ... dicimus aliquid necesse esse aut non esse in deo, non intelligitur quod sit in illo necessitas aut cogens aut prohibens* (*loc. cit.*) 'When ... we assert that something is necessary or not necessary in God this is not to be taken as implying that some coercive or prohibitive necessity operates on him'.

It is not made clear here whether this deprecation also extends to the attribution of necessary *existence* to God, and doubts may be raised on this score by an appeal to the various occasions, especially in the *Reply*, when phrases such as *necesse est illud esse* 'it is necessary that it should be', *ex necessitate est* 'he is of necessity', and so on, are used in respect of God. However, it is in most cases possible to construe these as expressions of that *necessitas non cogens* 'non-cogent necessity', that necessity which is embodied in a logical consequence, and is distinguished by Anselm in *Cur Deus Homo* II 17. This is the *necessitas consequentiae* 'inferential necessity' of the later medievals (cf. *HL* §5.691). Even in those cases wherein it is difficult to put such a construction upon these phrases, it appears highly doubtful that Anselm would approve of their being taken literally. Sentences attributing necessary existence to God can be shown to possess highly undesirable features from an Anselmian point of view. Given the equation, taken over from Boethius and accepted by Anselm, of *necesse esse* 'necessary to be' with *non posse non esse* 'not possible not to be', the predication of this last expression, either with or without the interposed *cogitari* 'to-be-thought' mentioned above, yields sentences such as *Deus non potest non esse* 'God is not able to be', and *Deus non potest cogitari non esse* 'God is not capable of being thought not to be'. Now it is clear from *Proslogion* 7, *De Veritate* 8, *De Casu Diaboli* 12 and other writings (*HL* §5.6) that for Anselm a sentence of the form 'X *non potest* . . .' 'X is not able . . .' ascribes, strictly speaking, an incapacity or liability to the X in question. When, therefore, the X is God, a reformulation ascribing the incapacity to its true subject has to be operated on the sentence. For instance, following the lines suggested in *De Casu Diaboli* 12, the first of the two sentences would become *Nulla res potest facere non esse deum* 'No thing is able to bring it about that God is not' and the second would become *Nullus homo potest cogitare quia deus non est* 'No human being is capable of thinking that God does not exist'. (This latter interpretation is in any case extractable from the text of *Proslogion* 4.) Thus any Anselmian ascription of necessary existence to God which proved to involve anything more than *necessitas consequentiae* 'inferential necessity' would turn out to be a mere concession to *usus loquendi* 'ordinary speech', ultimately corrigible in the way described, which accords with Anselm's general practice. The incapacity to think (in the appropriate sense of 'think') that God is not, made explicit by the second of the two analyses just given, has as its immediate source the intelligent following through of the *reductio ad absurdum* proof contained in ch. 3, or of alternative analyses exemplified in Anselm's *Reply*. Its ultimate source, however, is the *summa veritas* 'supreme truth' described in *De Veritate* 10 as the cause of the 'truth of thought' (*Causa est veritatis quae cogitationis est*).

This last-mentioned point is perhaps one of the reasons for the consequential structure of the first sentence of ch. 3 (4.1, repeated 4.4, 4.51), first noted above in connection with Gaunilo's contribution. The 'truth of thought' embodied in the incapacity to think of God as non-existent is the consequence of the 'truth of being' of the 'nature' whose existence has been proved in *Proslogion* 2. On this supposition it follows, therefore, that while the material of *Proslogion* 3 is not intended as a proof of the *existence* of God, it brings out the conditions under which an argument for God's *non-existence* could proceed. For the hypothetical, 'If God exists then God cannot be thought not to be' is plainly presupposed in ch. 3 as the implicit major premiss for a *modus ponendo ponens* argument based on the affirmation of that hypothetical's antecedent. Thus *sic vere est ut nec cogitari possit non esse* 'so truly does he exist that he cannot even be thought not to be' (4.1) states the minor and the conclusion of that argument; the minor itself (i.e. the proposition stating that God exists) has been deduced in ch. 2. Now the assumption of the same hypothetical, along with a minor stating the possibility of God's being thought not to be, would constitute a *modus tollendo tollens* argument having as its conclusion the statement that God does not exist. (St Anselm was, of course, fully acquainted with arguments of this form: cf. *HL* §9.)

Now, therefore, every point that has been raised above can be made to take its place in a coherent pattern. In *Proslogion* 2 the *existence* of God is in question (*es sicut credimus* 'you are, as we believe you are'); in *Proslogion* 3 the first of a whole series of divine attributes is being investigated (*hoc es quod credimus* 'you are what we believe you are'), but it is a most important attribute in the sense that its establishment is such as to preclude a proof of God's *non-existence* which, upon Anselm's own principles, would otherwise be possible. At the same time he is now committed to a description of the way in which the fool of the Psalms can *apparently* (but not really) think God not to be. This in turn links up with Anselm's whole view of linguistic analysis (*HL* §2.12). It is in *Proslogion* 4 that this link is to be found; it will not be pursued here.

Having thus established that the argument for the existence of God contained in Anselm's *Proslogion*, and known, since Kant, as the Ontological Argument, was originally conceived as belonging exclusively to ch. 2 of that work, we may now confine our attention to that chapter with the strictly limited objective of exploring a suggestion that emerges obviously enough from the use of the unrestricted quantification described in §2.252 of Part II. The argument of that chapter takes the form of a *reductio ad absurdum* proof which turns upon the apparent contradiction contained in 3.221. The latter, if taken to be of the form '$\sim (x$ is $x)$', is a contradiction only when interpreted relatively to the usual (restricted) type of quantification, whereas the unrestricted quantification described in II §2.252 allows the reading of this same form as merely an assertion that x does not exist. Now since we are in the context of the problem as to whether a certain object exists, it is clearly undesirable to analyse the proof in terms of a logic for which 'Everything exists' is a theorem (cf. II §2.2524); unrestricted quantification is therefore preferable. But this immediately admits the possibility just adumbrated, namely that what might *appear* to be a contradiction (relative to restricted quantifica-tion) is in fact *not* a contradiction, but a mere unstartling repetition of a premiss earlier fed into the argument (3.20) to the effect that the being in question does not exist (since it is in the intellect *alone*). Under these circumstances what *appear* to be the premisses of a *reductio ad absurdum* argument become a simple truism. What follows is for the most part an elaboration of this possibility. It will, however, have a couple of interesting byproducts: (i) a suggestion as to what can properly be understood by Kant's *dictum* so often quoted when the Ontological Argument is in question, i.e. that 'existence is not a predicate'; (ii) a new criticism based on the actual text of the original argument.

A further inspection of *Proslogion* 2 shows that Anselm is there dealing with two things: (i) questions of being and non-being, and (ii) a being's being in the understanding. Now (i) is coverable by the Ontology of which we have hitherto made use in this Part, whereas (ii) lays the way open to a bewildering multitude of interpretations. When someone is said to *understand* something, or to *have it in thought*, such a statement can be interpreted in at least three ways: psychological, epistemological, and logical. Psychologically, it is about the person who is doing the understanding, epistemologically it may raise questions as to the presuppositions demanded by the person's capacity to understand or think, while it is of logical interest in various ways. One such way exploits the fact that a statement of the sort in question tells us something about a theory (inchoate and fragmentary though it may be) which is being entertained by that person. Very heavy backing for this interpretation in an Anselmian context comes from his own lengthy discussions in the earlier chapters of *De Grammatico*. Passages well worth lengthier examination in this connection make it clear that for him discourse concerned with a thing's *being understood* is reducible to statements about the *esse* 'being' of a thing, and that these in turn are definitionally founded. It would hence appear not to be grossly misleading either in general or in relation to the interpretation of Anselm, were one to adopt the following as an interpretational postulate:

P: If the *a* is in the understanding then some theory is concerned with the *a*

Already this seems to give us something of what we want. Assuming the term '*a*' to be nominal, there is no incompatibility at all between its occurrence in a theory and its being an empty term (as required e.g. by 3.121 and the *in solo intellectu* 'in the understanding alone' parts of 3.20 and 3.21). The system of Ontology outlined in Part II is a concrete demonstration of this fact. In particular, use of the definitional frame shown at II §4.2.2 allows us to introduce a name 'n' in such a way that while one can say that the theory is concerned with n, there is no entailment that n exists. This possibility runs parallel to that of saying that n is in the understanding but without any commitment to the existence of n (cf. 3.1). It is plain from 3.132 that the antecedent of P above could also read 'the a is understood'. Thus far, therefore, we have the machinery necessary for covering the material of ch. 2 which is contained in the preliminary considerations numbered 3.10 to 3.132.

We now also have the means available for a minimal appreciation of Anselm's actual argument (3.2–3.4), in the sense that we can display a theory θ which embodies the term 'the being than which a greater cannot be thought' and the various suppositions of being and non-being therein deployed by Anselm. θ may in fact be constructed from the Ontology of Part II extended by the introduction of the term 'X' as an abbreviation of 'that being than which a greater cannot be thought'. Thus, since we are concerned with being and negation, let us first recall the axiom for Ontology, the functors of existence, and the definition of nominal negation. These constitute the opening phases of theory θ.

T1(= A1) $[ab] :: a \in b . \equiv : . [\exists c] . c \in a : . [c] : c \in a . \supset .$
$c \in b : . [cd] : c \in a . d \in a . \supset . c \in d$

T2(= D1) $[a] : . \text{sol}(a) . \equiv : [bc] : b \in a . c \in a . \supset . b \in c$

T3(= D2) $[a] : \text{ob}(a) . \equiv . [\exists b] . a \in b$

T4(= D3) $[a] : \text{ex}(a) . \equiv . [\exists b] . b \in a$

T5(= D4) $[ab] : a \in ʍ(b) . \equiv . a \in a . \sim (a \in b)$

And now, abbreviating *ens quo maius cogitari nequit* 'being than which a greater cannot be thought' by 'X', let us suppose there has been added to θ an axiom which introduces the term 'X', and which has as a consequence:

T6 $[a] :: a \in X . \supset : . a \in a : . [bc] : b \in X . c \in X . \supset .$
$b \in c$

There is no need for the present to occupy ourselves with the question of what is involved in being an X. As far as it goes, T6 merely ensures that there is at most one X, i.e. that 'X' is a singular term (cf. T2). In T6 we now have the correlate (by P) of the assertion which occurs several times in the Anselmian text, namely that the X is in the understanding. We can now go on to deduce some theses of Ontology which concern existence in general, and other theses which embody the term 'X' and functors of existence. Here we have the counterpart of understanding X's status in relation to existence without, however, understanding

X to exist. For instance, T7 which now follows is a reminder that there is no such thing as a non-existent X, and the many and various substitutions possible in others of the theorems deduced would enable one to expatiate on X's existence without at all presupposing the existence of X. This also shows how it is possible for the existence of something to be understood without it being understood that that thing exists:

T7	$[a]: a \in X . \supset . ex(X)$	(T4)
T8	$[a]: a \in X . \supset . sol(X)$	(T6, T2)
T9	$[a]: a \in X . \supset . ex(X) . sol(X)$	(T7, T8)

T10 $[a]: ex(a) . sol(a) . \supset . a \in a$
   $[a]::$
 (1) $ex(a) .$
 (2) $sol(a) . \supset:.$
 (3) $[\exists b] . b \in a :.$ (T4, 1)
 (4) $[bc]: b \in a . c \in a . \supset . b \in c :.$ (T2, 2)
  $a \in a$ (T1, 3, 4)

T11	$[a]: a \in X . \supset . X \in X$	(T9, T10)

T12 $[a]: a \in a . \supset . ex(a)$
   $[a]:.$
 (1) $a \in a . \supset:$
 (2) $[\exists b] . b \in a :$ (1)
  $ex(a)$ (T4, 2)

T13 $[a]: a \in a . \supset . sol(a)$
   $[a]::$
 (1) $a \in a . \supset:.$
 (2) $[bc]: b \in a . c \in a . \supset . b \in c :.$ (T1, 1)
  $sol(a)$ (T2, 2)

T14	$[a]: a \in a . \supset . ex(a) . sol(a)$	(T12, T13)
T15	$[a]: a \in a . \equiv . ex(a) . sol(a)$	(T10, T14)
T16	$[a]: ex(a) . sol(a) . \supset . ob(a)$	(T3, T10)
T17	$[a]: ob(a) . \supset . ex(a) . sol(a)$	(T3, T14)
T18	$[a]: ob(a) . \equiv . ex(a) . sol(a)$	(T16, T17)
T19	$[a]: a \in a . \equiv . ob(a)$	(T15, T18)

In order to partly appreciate the contrast between X's being in the understanding only and X's existing in fact (3.21) and in order to make the posit covered by 3.22, let us now add X's non-existence as an axiom and observe the results. Whatever else the 'X is in the understanding only' of 3.22 may mean, it at least has 'X does not exist'

as part of its import. There also follow a few theorems which ensue
from this posit:

T20(= A2)	$\sim (ex(X))$	
T21	$\sim (X \in X)$	(T20, T15)
T22	$[a] : a \in X . \supset . X \in X . \sim (X \in X)$	(T11, T21)
T23	$[a] : a \in X . \supset . X \in {\scriptstyle N} (X)$	(T5, T22)
T24	$[a] . \sim (a \in X)$	(T23)

Here we have a sketch of what can legitimately be inferred from the
supposition of X's non-existence (3.22). Unlike Anselm, however, we
have been able to obtain the apparent contradiction (T21) without
having to take into account the considerations concerning 'more
great' (3.21) from which Anselm derives *his* contradiction (3.221). For
Anselm himself clearly believes that 'that very being than which a
more great is not able to be thought is that than which a more great
is able to be thought' (3.221) is contradictory, as 3.3 shows ('This
cannot be'). Let us now pause to consider the import of 3.221, the
apparent contradiction in question. Our first task is to relate it to
its counterparts in the systematic background provided by θ, the
second to check on whether it is or is not contradictory, and the third
to decide what the effects of an interpretation of it as contradictory
may be.

From the point of view of θ, 3.221 has in fact two interpretations;
as it stands in the text it appears to be of the form 'X is not-X', but at
the corresponding point in *Proslogion* 3 the contradiction which is used
to found a similar *reductio ad absurdum* proof reads, 'that very thing
than which a greater is not able to be thought is not that than which a
greater is not able to be thought' (4.31), and this, while still susceptible
of being read as of the 'X is not-X' form, might also be interpreted
as 'X is-not X', i.e. as 'It is false that X is X'. Let us first attribute
this latter interpretation to 3.221. If *this* is what is meant, then as far
as θ is concerned, we do not have a contradiction here. As becomes
evident from a consideration of T19 and T6, we merely have in a
new form that part of the earlier premiss (3.22, cf. T20) which by
its use of 'in the understanding *only*' asserts the non-existence of X.
In systematic terms, 3.221 merely records in its own way that T21
can be inferred from T20, and T21 is certainly not a contradiction.
Under this interpretation, therefore, the *reductio* cannot proceed;
there is no contradiction, and hence no negation of antecedent suppositions which have contradiction as their consequence. Anselm will,
however, be in quite distinguished company in thinking that 'X is
not X' *must* be contradictory. Anyone who takes '*a* is *a*' to be a thesis,
as do the restricted quantificationalists, would likewise label '*a* is not
a' as contradictory. In fact, as θ with its unrestricted quantification

9

has demonstrated, '*a* is not *a*' *can* be interpreted as simply denying that *a* exists. In view of T20 this is just what one would expect.

Next, let the interpretation of 'X is not X' which *is* a contradiction be considered; this will be of the form 'X ∈ *N*(X)' and its contradictory nature is evident from T5(= D4). Now θ, as exposed above, certainly agrees with 3.22 and 3.221 in granting that if X is in the understanding *only*, then 'X is not-X' comes out somewhere, but not in quite the same position as that in which Anselm requires it to be. By *P*, 'X is in the understanding *only*' means that the term 'X' has been introduced into θ (T6), and that 'X does not exist' has been added as an axiom (T20(= A2)). The salient consequences of these facts, as θ shows, are T11 and T21 respectively, which when combined yield T22, and this by T5(= D4) gives T23. Examination of the latter will show that 'X is not-X' is not a full statement of the consequence of the supposition suggested at 3.22, but is rather itself the contradictory consequent of a hypothetical consequence. And the only inference which can be based on the contradictory nature of the consequent of T23 is the negation of the antecedent of that same T23, a negation which is shown in T24, and which amounts to the assertion that nothing is X. Interpreted in this way, Anselm's argument merely proves the truism that if the term '*a*' is introduced in θ, and *a*'s existence denied in θ, then a hypothetical proposition with a contradictory consequent can be inferred. The ensuing negation of the antecedent by *modus tollendo tollens* merely amounts to a reiteration of the already posited denial of *a*'s existence. Further, θ itself indicates how *any* nominal term could take the place of 'X' and yield the same results.

In short, having followed a procedure which mimics that of Anselm, one can in the first place admit that the introduction of 'X' into θ (i.e. into the understanding, cf. *P*) commits us to the hypothetical existence of X, so that we have theorems such as T7, T8, and T9. However, without even entering into Anselm's notion that an existing X is greater than a non-existing one (3.21), and merely by adding an axiom (T20, 3.21) stating that X does not exist, one can then deduce that X is-not X as in T21 (cf. 3.221). This latter is not in fact a contradiction, but merely a reiteration that X does not exist. The contradiction required for the purposes of his argument, i.e. 'X is not-X', is not deducible, save as the consequent of a theorem such as T23 which (as T24 illustrates) merely amounts to a further repetition of the supposition of X's non-existence (T20). Considerations concerning 'greater than' are hence otiose, since whether they intervene or not, these results still follow.

It may well still be contended that the vital point in Anselm's argument, namely the sense of 'more great' in 3.21, on which hinges the 'on this account' of 3.22, having thus been ignored, the original argument may, for all we know, still be valid. However, we are now in a position to realise that whether the existence of X be denied or affirmed in θ, the content of that term is not thereby changed in such a way as to produce (or fail to produce) the contradiction (3.221) used to found the *reductio* argument. The addition of T20 to θ just cannot bring it about that X becomes or is non-X. (This is, I take it, part of what Kant meant when he said in this connection that 'existence is not a predicate'. At any rate it is a more feasible gloss than that given by the upholders of restricted quantification who arrogate to themselves the august associations of that dictum on grounds quite remote from those envisaged by Kant, i.e. because of their interpretation of the 'existential' quantifier; cf. II §2.25.)

Moreover, if contrary to this acceptable sense of the Kantian dictum, one does grant that adding T20 (or its negation) to θ does make a difference to the content of 'X', then this is quite fatal to the original aim of the argument in that it can then just as feasibly be used to prove the impossibility of X's existence. This becomes clear when the hitherto missing thread, i.e. the 'more great' of 3.20, is considered. Anselm holds that confining that-than-which-a-greater-cannot-be-thought to the understanding makes it 'less great' than it is if it is also in reality. But if (as is clear from 3.110, 3.130, 3.4, and so on) he holds that this being-than-which-a-more-great-cannot-be-thought is at least in the understanding, then on similar grounds he should also admit that it cannot exist in reality, since this would entail its being more great than that-than-which-a-greater-cannot-be thought, which is impossible. The alleged possibility of thought ('it can be thought also to exist in fact') mentioned in 3.21 becomes an impossibility. One can think of nothing greater than the greatest.

Hence on his own principles the vital section of the argument which we have been considering could equally well (or even more feasibly) read:

3.20   It is certain that that-than-which-a-more-great-cannot-be-thought must only be in the understanding.

3.21   For if it is at least in the understanding, it cannot be thought also to exist in fact, since this would be more great.

3.22   On this account if that-than-which-a-more-great-cannot-be-thought exists in fact, then

3.221 that very thing than which a more great is *not* able to be thought is that than which a more great *is* able to be thought.

3.3   But obviously this (3.221) cannot be.

3.4   Hence without any doubt something-than-which-a-more-great-is-not-able-to-be-thought cannot exist both in the understanding and in fact.

9*

§8   ABELARD ON INCREASE

Prologue: HUME AND A BROOM

One day Hume, while walking up the steps of his club, received an unusually lively impression of being tumbled back down to the street by the vigorous action of a sweeper with a broom. The sweeper hastened to the bottom of the steps and helped the philosopher to his feet.

'Begging your pardon, sir!' he said, pulling off his cap, 'But I was thinking about my broom, as you might say, and how it's served me these thirty years, so I didn't see you coming, sir.'

Hume perceived the broom and observed that it was remarkably well-preserved, considering its daily employment over thirty years. The sweeper raised his cap again—perhaps to Hume, or possibly out of respect for the broom.

'Yes, sir!' he said, 'That's on account of the new 'ead. You see, sir, I gives it a new 'ead every summer.' He replaced his cap.

'Nevertheless,' said Hume, 'the handle is likewise in excellent condition. Quite remarkable!'

'Yes, sir,' said the sweeper, removing his cap—this time to knock the dust from Hume's hose, 'That'll be on account of the new 'andle I gives it every winter.'

'Come, come, my good man!' smiled Hume, 'We can only attribute identity to this broom provided all the parts continue uninterruptedly and invariably the same.' It was charming to observe the mental confusions of the lower orders.

The fellow did, indeed, seem perplexed.

'All the parts, sir?' He made as if to remove his cap, but it was already off. 'But not all, sir. After all, if it loses a bristle . . ..'

'If some small or inconsiderable part be added to the mass,' Hume explained kindly, 'or be subtracted from it: though this absolutely destroys the identity of the whole, strictly speaking, yet as we seldom think so accurately, we scruple not to pronounce a mass of matter the same, where we find so trivial an alteration.'

The sweeper replaced his cap, visibly cheered.

'You 'ad me worried for a minute, sir! I likes to think it's the same broom been 'anded down, father to son . . ..'

''Tis the proportion of the change that counts', said Hume, taking a pinch of snuff to soothe his rising irritation. How tiresome these fellows could be! 'A broom cannot undergo a change amounting to one half of its mass and preserve its identity. You would have to supply good reasons indeed to call it the same.'

'But I've always used it for the same job, this broom. Steps and *portico. You won't find me using it for the 'all or the street. No sir! This is the steps broom: always 'as been.'*

'I'll grant you,' said Hume, *'a combination of the parts to some common end or purpose lends weight to your claim. The common end, in which the parts conspire, is the same under all their variations, and affords an easy transition of the imagination from one situation of the body to another.'* Hume had for some time suspected that Locke had distant relations among the lower classes. Here, peradventure, was one of them.

'And it's always been kept in the same place,' insisted the sweeper, *'under the servants' stairs.'*

'Indeed!' said Hume.

'And it's always been used by the same person. No one else touches it, sir; not this broom.'

'No doubt!' Hume began to mount the steps again, but was accosted by the sweeper at the top. The fellow had again removed his cap and, in his eagerness, handed it to Hume, thus freeing both hands with which he gripped the broom violently. Hume took the cap without noticing, so upset was he by this time.

'The 'andle wouldn't be no use without the 'ead, would it, sir? And the 'ead wouldn't be no use by itself, if I may put it so bold,' said the sweeper. The philosopher muttered something about *'sympathy of parts'* and said *''Pon my soul!'*, though he knew this to be without significance. Then, to hide his feelings, he tried to take snuff from the sweeper's cap.

'See here, my good fellow!' he said, determined to settle the matter. *' You have a distinct idea of that broom handle which remains invariable until such time as it wears out. Whereupon you change it.'* The sweeper nodded. Hume continued, *' You have also a distinct idea of several different objects, namely the old broom handles and heads and their replacements, existing in succession, and connected together by a close relation.'* He paused to hand the sweeper his cap. *'This, my good man, affords as perfect a notion of diversity as if there were no manner of relation among the objects.'* He paused again, and the sweeper nodded.

''Tis certain,' Hume concluded, *'that in your common way of thinking, the former idea of identity or sameness is confounded with the latter idea of diversity.'* He turned towards the club door. Dr Mandeville and Mr Hutcheson would have set up the backgammon board by now, and would not like to be kept waiting. *'Good day to you!'* he said, and tossed the sweeper a coin.

'One moment, sir!' said the sweeper. *'If I may be so bold, sir. Tell me then, is the 'andle the broom, or is the 'ead the broom? If the 'ead's the broom or the 'andle's the broom, then this broom is two brooms, and at the same time 'alf a broom.'*

'It is indeed!' said Hume, who was beginning to be worried, for he suspected that he might have tossed the fellow a whole penny by mistake. Confound him!

(David Mannings)

As will become evident below, Abelard was vexed by somewhat the same puzzles as are attributed to Hume in this amusing passage. This is because these thinkers probably have in common a thesis which was certainly and consistently maintained by Abelard throughout his treatment of the theory of parts and wholes, namely that *no thing has more or less parts at one time than at another* (*AD* 423.29.31, *AP* 300.20.21, and cf. 'Hume''s remarks on the bristles). This is, in Abelard's treatment, coupled with what may for present purposes be called the Paradox of Increase: it is impossible for anything to increase by the addition of parts, since when further parts are adjoined to a thing, neither that to which the parts are adjoined, nor the adjoined parts themselves, increase in the sense that they have more parts than they had before (*AD* 421.35.37, *AP* 299.19.30). What then can be made of the way in which both ordinary usage and logic appear to countenance increase? (*AD* 423.19.22). In the *Logica 'Ingredientibus'* Abelard concludes that talk about increase is best confined to those cases wherein the initial and terminal states of the alleged process are of the same sort. Thus the addition of stones to a *heap of stones* yields a *heap of stones*, the addition of pieces of wood to a *heap* of stones still yields a *heap*, but we have no word to identify the result of adding men to the heap of stones. In this last instance, therefore, according to Abelard talk about increase is out of place, or at least presents a problem. At the same time, and in the same work, he deprecates the inclusion of the notion of *increase in the number of parts* in any elucidation of increase. It is the production of a like-natured composite, rather than increase in part-numbers, which constitutes the essence of increase (*AP* 300.17.20). Now it is quite evident that this verdict fails to answer the question: *what is it* that (according to the ordinary view) increases? All we have is the replacement of one state of affairs by another of the same sort, as in the case of 'Hume''s description of the progress of the sweeper's broom. Again, the implication that increase in the number of parts is somehow secondary is plainly unsatisfactory, since this would ordinarily be thought essential to any account of quantitative increase. Indeed, Abelard himself appears to have sensed that an account of increase which would remedy these defects was still required, and such an account is attempted in his *Dialectica* (*AD* 421–424). There, as we shall see, he attempts to give an account of increase which allows a place to the addition of parts; in so doing, however, he still fails to adequately resolve the paradox. In the course of the comments which now follow it will be suggested that one basis of its solution may be found in certain other portions of his extensive remarks on parts and wholes. The other basis lies in a distinction of which both he and the 'Hume' of our prologue fail to make use, namely that between (i) being part-of-an-object and (ii) being an object-part. This distinction will be enlarged on below.

Before proceeding to the *Dialectica* passage, however, some clarification of the logical nature of the field within which these topics lie is obviously appropriate. It only needs the addition to the Ontology of Part II of a further single primitive term ('proper part') to bring us into the region of the 'collective classes' (or 'complete collections') of Leśniewski's *Mereology* (cf. *SM* and *LLL* 4.9, 4.10). Such complete collections are the literal totality of all the elements which go to compose them. Thus the collective class of states-in-the-United-States has as its parts not only an element such as Rhode Island (which happens to be a state-in-the-United-States) but also the city of New Orleans, the southernmost rock of Cape Cod, and, in general, any arbitrarily selected segment (whether continuous or discrete) of the whole which is the United States. As a result, one of the distinguishing features of the collective class or complete collection is that among its elements may be things other than the sort of thing overtly mentioned in the specification of the class. Thus although Rhode Island is an element of the class of states-in-the-United-States and *is* also a state-in-the-United-States, its fellow element New Orleans is not a state, although like all its fellow parts, it has at least a part in common with a state (cf. the definition .4 below). With collective classes may be contrasted classes regarded in the distributive sense. These are such that every element (or 'member') thereof *is* a thing of the sort associated with the class-name. Thus to say that Socrates is a member of the class of men (in the distributive sense) simply amounts to saying that Socrates is a man.

Now Abelard was well aware of the distinction between distributive wholes (e.g. species) and collective wholes, both continuous (e.g. a bronze rod, a house) and discrete (e.g. a flock, a gaggle, a people, duos, quartets, sextets, and so on); indeed 'continuous' and 'discrete' are terms used by him in this connection (*AD* 547.28). Collective wholes are called by him 'integral' or 'constitutive', as well as 'conjunctive' (*AD* 546.26, *AD* 547.27, *AD* 339.32), although he deprecates the use of the term 'collective' in connection with certain non-discrete wholes (*AD* 431–2). Distributive wholes are called by him 'universal' and 'general', as well as 'distributive' (*secundum diffusionem*) (*AD* 546.26.27, *AD* 339.31). And although he studies both sorts of wholes, both severally and comparatively, his appreciation in *Logica*

'*Ingredientibus*' of the collective ('*collectio*') as a possible theory of universals is vitiated by his lack of the distinction between a collective class proper (cf. .4 below) and a mere collection (as opposed to a complete collection) (cf. .11 below).

To the Ontology outlined in Part II one may add a further single primitive term, namely '*ppt*( )', readable as 'proper part of . . .'. This term is a functor which forms a name from a name or name-like expression, and its import may be informally explained by saying that while in an 'improper' sense every object is a part of itself (i.e. is that part which is identical with the whole object) no object is a proper part of itself (cf. .1 below). Alternatively, there is a sense of 'part' embracing both the 'improper' sense (according to which an object *is* a part of itself) and the 'proper' sense of the word (cf. 3. below). The reading 'proper part' is designed to exclude this broad sense, for which the alternative nomenclature 'element' may be used, and which (as .3 shows) can in its turn be defined in terms of identity and 'proper part'. Leśniewski's original axiom system (1916) for Mereology was framed in terms of the notion of proper part, and may be expressed as follows:

.1 $[ab] : a \in ppt(b) . \supset . b \in N\,(ppt(a))$

.2 $[abc] : a \in ppt(b) . b \in ppt(c) . \supset . a \in ppt(c)$

.3 $[ab] :. a \in pt(b) . \equiv : a = b . \lor . a \in ppt(b)$

.4 $[ab] :: a \in ccl(b) . \equiv :. a \in a : [\exists c] . c \in b :.[c] : c \in b . \supset .$
           $c \in pt(a) :. [c] : c \in pt(a) . \supset . [\exists de] . d \in b . e \in pt(c) .$
           $e \in pt(d)$

.5 $[abc] : a \in ccl(c) . b \in ccl(c) . \supset . a \in b$

.6 $[ab] : a \in b . \supset . [\exists c] . c \in ccl(b)$

Although intuitively advantageous, this system has a certain inelegance in the sense that .3 and .4 are definitions which are in turn used in axioms .5 and .6. Later axiomatisations avoid these and other defects (cf. *SM* and *LM*). The sense of .1 and of .2 is clear enough. Definition .3 introduces 'part' in the broad sense (alternatively 'element'). The functor '*pt*( )' therein defined may hence be read as 'proper or improper part of . . .' or as 'element of . . .'. Definition .4 introduces the notion of collective class (or complete collection), indicated by '*ccl*( )'. Thus *a* is the collective class of *b*'s if and only if *a* exists, *b*'s exist, every *b* is a proper or improper part of *a*, and every proper or improper part of *a* has a proper or improper part in common with a *b*. Axiom .5 lays it down that there is only one collective class of a given set of objects, while .6 says that if there are *b*'s then there is the totality, the collective class, of *b*'s.

From the axioms and definitions presented a few simple theses may
be derived, e.g.

.7	$[ab]:a\in ppt(b)\,.\supset.\,b\in b$	(.1)
.8	$[ab]:a\in ppt(b)\,.\supset.\sim(b\in ppt(a))$	(.1)
.9	$[a]\,.\sim(a\in ppt(a))$	(.8)
.10	$[ab]:a\in ppt(b)\,.\supset.\sim(a\in b)$	(.7,\ .9)

It is from .10 that we may derive an answer to the final question posed
by the sweeper of our *Prologue*: the handle is not the broom, nor is
the head the broom, since in general, if *a* is a proper part of *b*, then
it is not the case that *a* is *b*. The definition of 'collection of . . .' (as
opposed to the 'complete collection of . . .' defined in .4) runs as
follows:

.11 $[ab]::a\in cl(b)\,.\equiv:.\,a\in a:.\,[c]:c\in pt(a)\,.\supset.$
         $[\exists de]\,.\,d\in b\,.\,d\in pt(a)\,.\,e\in pt(c)\,.\,e\in pt(d)$

It may be noted that this definition resembles .4 except insofar as there
is no guarantee written into its *definiens* ensuring that *every* *b* is a
part of *a*. There may thus be *b*'s outside a given collection of *b*'s.
Abelard's objections against using the theory of collective classes as
one solution to the problem of universals (*AP* 14.32–15.22) either
involve bringing out the very properties of collective classes (i.e.
complete collections) which differentiate them from distributive
classes or (as already remarked) involve confusion between a complete collection and a mere collection. Any group of men taken together (*quoslibet plures homines simul acceptos*) is only a mere collection and hence, as Abelard rightly says, not a candidate for an
alternative theory of universals. However, at this point he fails to
realise how a *complete* collection could offer such an alternative
account. Such are the beginnings of a theory of parts and wholes which
could be used to elucidate many of Abelard's vastly extensive remarks
on such matters. The section of those remarks with which we are at
present concerned, however, can be depicted as having more to do
with the applications of Mereology (i.e. with what shall be taken to
be the substituends for the variables in particular instances) than with
further ramifications of that theory. Full formal treatment of the
problem of increase would in fact require an excursion into Chronology (theory of time) as a supplement to Mereology.

In order to deal more briefly with Abelard's attempts, in the
Dialectica, to do justice to the notion of increase, it will suffice to pursue
the matter only in so far as the sorts of parts and wholes of which he
speaks may be broadly distinguished. Thus the distinction mentioned
earlier as lacking in Abelard's treatment may now be approached as

follows. In accordance with the policy suggested in *Logica 'Ingredienti-bus'* and described above, he uses as an example the quadrilateral that 'becomes' a larger quadrilateral by the addition of the former's gnomon (i.e. the L-shaped figure composed of three quadrilaterals each the same size as the original one). One thus has an increase whose initial and terminal states are of the same quadrilateral nature. Looking at the process from the point of view of the larger quadrilateral (i.e. the terminal whole) one may say that it consists of those objects which are *parts of* the larger quadrilateral (i.e. *parts of* that terminal whole) and which were formerly larger-quadrilateral *parts* (i.e. terminal-whole *parts*). This distinction between *parts of* an object, and object-*parts* is the vital supplement which becomes clear when it is considered that parts can only be *parts of* an object when incorporated in an object which actually exists. When, for example, the parts are not yet assembled, they are only object-*parts*. Compare the distinction between automobile parts and parts of an automobile, between broom-parts and parts of a broom. This distinction, which might be called the nominative/genitive distinction, is due to Czesław Lejewski. True, there are places at which Abelard appears to be stressing the genitive and other aspects of this distinction (*AD* 547.31–548.10, *AD* 343.32–346.28), but this is not always clear. In any case, he signally fails to make use of it, a failure paralleled in other portions of the present field, as will be made explicit below.

Thus armed, we may now turn to the *Dialectica* passage (*AD* 421–424), the aim of which, as already indicated, is to give an account of *increase* which will involve the whole's being made to have more parts, and yet at the same time preserve the basic thesis that no thing has more or less parts at one time than at another. Abelard also attempts to solve the problem: *what is it* that increases? In the course of these exercises he enunciates the counterparts of certain of the mereological theses given above. Nevertheless it will be found that not only is his treatment of the problem bedevilled by his neglect of the distinction made in the last paragraph, but also by a basic equivocation. Indeed, it is this equivocation which causes the *Dialectica* text to be immensely puzzling at first reading. It would appear, he says, that no increase can take place in something by the conjoining to it of something else. When one thing is conjoined to another, then neither that which is conjoined nor that to which it is conjoined increase, since neither has more parts than it previously had. Yet neither does the whole which is composed of these various parts increase. It still keeps only those parts which it previously had. For even as the two (namely the adjoined and that to which it is adjoined) when combined form together a whole in relation to each part, so also when disjoined these were the whole in relation to the *same parts*.

All the many parts, whether adjacent or disjoined, constitute the whole in relation to each of those parts. What then is it that increases? (*AD* 421.34–442.6). Thus far, this is a clear restatement of the Paradox of Increase mentioned at the outset of the present section. It is already evident that Abelard is attempting to work out his problem in terms of object-parts, and is neglecting the difference between them and parts-of-an-object.

The puzzles mentioned in the last paragraph begin when Abelard goes on to assert that increase should be said to be in the composite, as it has more parts (. . . *dicendum* (*est*) *augmentum esse in composito respectu simplicium, cum plures habeat partes, AD* 422.7.8). Now while one can immediately sense that the *having of more parts*, deliberately minimised as an essential feature of increase as described in *Logica 'Ingredientibus'* is here being brought to the fore, it is not at all apparent that he has resolved the various questions. The attribution of increase to the composite merely leaves the questions intact: the composite has not increased, and indeed was just not in existence previously, as he himself rightly reminds us on the next page (*primus namque compositum non erat, AD* 423.25). Hence that composite certainly does not have more parts than it previously had. He next elucidates increase (*augmentum*) with reference to the part/whole situation. *Augmentum*, he says, involves one thing's having all the parts of another thing, and some more besides, as in the relation of whole to part. All parts of the parts must be parts of the whole, and every whole must also be the sum of its parts (cf. .2 and .4 above). For as all the parts of each part also go to make up the whole itself, the whole must have quantitatively more parts than each of its several individual parts, that is to say, it embraces all those parts and has certain others as well, and this amounts to having more parts *in addition* (*plures in augmento partes habere*). This also involves having common parts which are essential to increase (*AD* 422.12.22).

Now while a great deal of what is here said about parts and wholes is acceptable in so far as it relates either to parts in general, or to object-parts, it is not at all clear how such material could constitute a solution to Abelard's problem. After all, as he himself pointed out earlier, a part/whole situation (in respect of *object-parts*, we may add) already existed before the increase; why, then, should these truisms about the more-partedness of the composite whole be invoked? And now we come to the equivocation which was mentioned above. The suspicion arises that Abelard is involved in a confusion based on the fact that a whole may be said to have all the parts of any one of its parts and some more *in addition*. Now clearly the use of 'in addition' (as in *plures in augmento partes habere* 'to have more parts in addition') involving as it does the word *augmentum* 'addition' need *not* imply that an *augmentum* (addition, increase) has taken place. Indeed, given his insistence on object-parts, all his preliminary arguments against such an event still stand. Owing, however, to the occurrence of the words 'additional parts' in both of the following two situation-descriptions:

(A) a whole's being made to have more, or additional, parts;
(B) a whole having more, or additional, parts being made to be;

he appears to be claiming that (B) is what really occurs when, in ordinary language, (A) is indicated. Now these two are plainly not equivalent. The first appears to be incompatible with Abelard's general thesis. The second is compatible with that thesis if we grant that the *compositum* (e.g. of rectangle and gnomon) is somehow a new object. Yet in view of his dealing with object-parts throughout, all the part/whole theses and the truths about parts in addition still held before the adjunction took place. And the question 'What is it that increases?' has still not been answered.

However, in the next phase of the discussion, after an unpromising start, it looks for a moment as though a more acceptable solution has almost been reached. Thus Abelard uses the already-mentioned example of the quadrilateral which 'becomes' a larger quadrilateral by the conjunction of its gnomon. The composite constructed from the original quadrilateral and the gnomon can be said to have increased, he claims, since the whole contains what any one of the parts contains plus whatever any of the other parts contain (*AD* 423.5.7). So far this is a mere exemplification of (B) above. Next, however, he succeeds in endowing 'having more parts' with a sense hitherto unexploited: to increase, he says, is, in respect of a given composite, to have more parts *in some place* than it had there before. Thus increase does not involve an aggregate's having more parts *simpliciter* (as in (A) above) nor is it to be whittled down to situation (B). Rather a given composite has, in the event of an increase, more quantitative parts in an appropriate place than it had earlier:

.12   For any composite to be increased, therefore, it must have more parts in some place than it formerly had in that place, and diminution involves having less than before. Increase occurs in relation to the extent of the bringing together of things in the same place, and does

Est igitur augeri quamlibet compositum plures partes ipsum habere in aliquo loco quam prius haberet in eodem, et diminui pauciores habere quam prius, ut secundum capacitatem et aggrega-tionem in in eumdem locum augmentum consistat, non tantum secundum plurali-

not just involve a greater number of parts. For the parts themselves are not greater in number; rather the composite has more parts *in this place* than it formerly had. Thus, should there be two men, one inside a house and one outside, these two are a composite in relation to each; if then the one who is outside is brought into the house, then that composite has more parts in the house than it had before, but it has not on that account more parts than it had before.

tatem partium. Ipsae namque partes plures non sunt, sed ipsum compositum plures partes habet in hoc loco quam prius. Veluti si duo sint homines, unus intra domum et unus extra, illi duo unum sunt compositum ad singulos, et si exterior in domum abstrahatur, idem compositum plures partes in domum habet quam prius: sed non ideo plures partes quam prius.

(*AD* 423.8.16)

In this way Abelard is able to preserve his original thesis, framed in terms of object-parts: for him there is now no question of an identical object's having more parts at one time than it has at another. Rather, an identical collection of object-parts has more of those parts in an appropriate place than it had at that place previously.

Abelard shows himself to be aware of the extent to which this verdict does not cohere with usage (which implies more parts *simpliciter*) or with logical authority (i.e. Boethius) according to whom the following is true:

If something is added to any thing, then the whole is made bigger.   (*AD* 423.22)

In elucidating this maxim he confirms his maintenance of a variant of (B) above. The maxim is not, he says, to be interpreted in the sense that a composite is made bigger than it previously was; rather a composite is made to be (which is) bigger than its individual parts by the adjoining of any one or other of those parts; formerly that composite just wasn't there (*AD* 423.23.25). It is these last words (*prius namque compositum non erat*) which suggest the maintenance of the following modification of (B):

(B₁): a whole having more parts *in this place* (or *appropriately placed*) being made to be.

And apparently it is to this new whole, consisting of duly-placed parts, that the appellation 'whole' (*totum*) properly applies, for he continues: the comparison involved in increase is not that between the composite and itself [since the original whole remains the same, whether its parts are in or out of place] but between the whole and its individual parts [they now stand in a new part/whole relation]. Hence he approves of Boethius' having used the word 'whole' (as opposed to e.g. 'that thing') in the maxim quoted above (*AD* 423.27.29).

In short, therefore, it is evident that although Abelard has made explicit certain truths which *do* hold in respect of increase of the sort in question, the only remotely feasible answer he has given to the problem of *what it is* that increases is that it is the *number of duly-placed parts* which increases. Throughout, by a sort of self-denying ordinance, he has insisted on talking in terms of object-parts, rather than also of parts-of-an-object. Abelard appears to think that such due placement, or the more-partedness of a newly-formed whole in relation to one or other of its component parts is the only viable interpretation of the usual association of increase with more-partedness

Nevertheless, there is ample material in his other discussions of increase, decrease, and of temporal wholes to allow the formulation of more feasible answers to the problem of what it is that increases, and yet at the same time preserve at least one sense of his thesis that no thing has more (or less) parts at one time than at another. Thus he asserts that removal of a pebble from the wall of a given house engenders a different house (and to this extent his thesis is preserved) but that one can nevertheless say that a house remains. Likewise, although Socrates with his fingernail and Socrates without his fingernail are not the same Socrates, we nevertheless continue to call him 'Socrates' and 'a human being' in both cases (*AD* 549–551). Again, he asserts that philosophers should treat a temporal whole (e.g. a day), consisting of several successive parts which are not simultaneously present, as if that whole were one and the same thing (*AD* 554). One need only apply this last idea to the two former examples in order to see that although in one of the senses required by Abelard's thesis one has a successive of different houses and different Socrateses, yet ordinarily one treats such successions as earlier and later temporal *parts-of-the-wholes* in question. The house considered as the whole of its temporal parts and Socrates considered as a whole of his temporal parts (earlier and later) *can* be said to have less (or more) parts at one time than at another. Here we are dealing with parts-of-the-house and parts-of-Socrates, as opposed to just house-parts which later become parts-of-the-house.

Likewise with Abelard's increasing quadrilateral: in one sense the successive additions of gnomons (object-parts) produce new objects (parts-of-an-object) having the part/whole relations ascribed to them by Abelard. Thus far, and thus far only his main thesis may be preserved, but the question as to what it is that increases does not receive a satisfactory answer. However, the successive stages thus produced can in turn be regarded as earlier and later temporal parts-of a single expanding object extended in time. It is *this* object which increases, and it is to this object, consisting of parts-of-an-object as opposed to object-parts, that Abelard's thesis does *not* apply. A road having different breadths at different points along its length is still the same road; an object extended in time but having diverse spatial dimensions owing to the adjoining of object-parts which become parts-of-the-object or because of the disjoining of parts-of-the-object which thereby become object-parts, is still the same object.

By thus focusing upon parts-of-an-object, and not allowing oneself to be distracted by the earlier or later career of such parts in their role of object-parts, commonsense and logic can preserve their attitudes towards increase and decrease without the untoward modifications proposed by Abelard, whose thesis that no object has more or less parts at one time than at another is now seen to be valid only in an unnecessarily limited sense. The same limitations may be shown to have caused Hume's opinions to differ from those of the broom-user.

INDEX

Only titles of writings not mentioned in the list of abbreviations (pp. xi–xiii) are included in this index.